Grade 2

Scott Foresman

On-Level
Take-Home Readers

ISBN: 0-328-16897-1
Copyright © Pearson Education, Inc.

Editorial Offices: Glenview, Illinois • Parsippany, New Jersey • New York, New York
Sales Offices: Boston, Massachusetts • Duluth, Georgia • Glenview, Illinois
Coppell, Texas • Sacramento, California • Mesa, Arizona

Contents

How to Use the Take-Home Leveled Readers

1. Tear out the pages for each Take-Home Leveled Reader. Make a copy for each child. Be sure to copy both sides of each page.

2. Fold the pages in half to make a booklet.

3. Staple the pages on the left-hand side.

4. Share the Take-Home Leveled Readers with children. Suggest they read these with family members.

Suggested levels for Guided Reading, DRA™, Lexile,® and Reading Recovery™ are provided in the Pearson Scott Foresman Leveling Guide.

Genre	Comprehension Skills and Strategy
Realistic fiction	• Character and Setting • Plot • Predict

Scott Foresman Reading Street 2.1.1

PEARSON
Scott Foresman

scottforesman.com

ISBN 0-328-13233-0

9 780328 132331

90000

The New Kid

by Eve Beck

illustrated by Nicole Wong

Word count: 278

Think and Share (Read Together)

1. What two settings are in this story?

2. Use a diagram like the one below to compare Denny's life in Bali and in California.

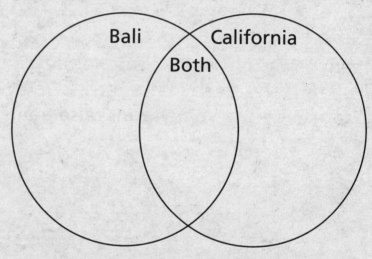

3. Choose a page from this story. On a separate piece of paper, make a list of words on your page that have a short vowel sound.

4. What do you think might be difficult about moving to a new country?

Farms Around the World

Read Together

In this story, you read that Denny's dad helped farmers in Bali. Did you know that there are farming communities all around the world? A farm is a place that grows plants or raises animals for food. In Indonesia, many farms grow rice crops. In the United States, many farms grow wheat crops. In Kenya, some farms raise goats for their milk.

Goat farm in Kenya

12

The New Kid

by Eve Beck

illustrated by Nicole Wong

PEARSON

Scott
Foresman

Editorial Offices: Glenview, Illinois • Parsippany, New Jersey • New York, New York
Sales Offices: Needham, Massachusetts • Duluth, Georgia • Glenview, Illinois
Coppell, Texas • Ontario, California • Mesa, Arizona

I remember Bali. I was the new kid there. It was somewhere that I was someone special. That makes me feel good.

11

Now I am back in California. I am in second grade. I fit in here. I dress like my friends. I eat with a knife and fork. The bathroom is down the hall.

But now I miss being the new kid.

My name is Denny. My dad helps out small farms. This summer we went to the country of Bali. That is an island in the Indian Ocean. Kids don't speak English there. They speak Indonesian. But we all know soccer.

My new friend Ketut taught me to say *makanan*. It means "food." Mom and Dad didn't learn any Indonesian words at first. I helped them out a lot.

There was a puppet show at the temple. It lasted all night long. I fell asleep. It was still the best night of our Bali summer.

4

9

In Bali, you go to a temple, not a church. Families drive motorcycles, not cars. Ketut's family took us to a temple.

The food there was good. We ate fried rice, chicken, and ice cream. And you can eat with your fingers. Everyone in Indonesia does that, except Mom and Dad.

In Bali our house was called a *rumah*.
The front door was a gate in a big wall.
We had a beautiful garden to play in.

In a *rumah* all the rooms stand alone. The kitchen is one building. The bathroom is another building. The living room has no walls. My bedroom was like my own little house. At first it was scary. But I started to like it.

Science

Science

Earth Science

Space Walk

by Ginny Grissom

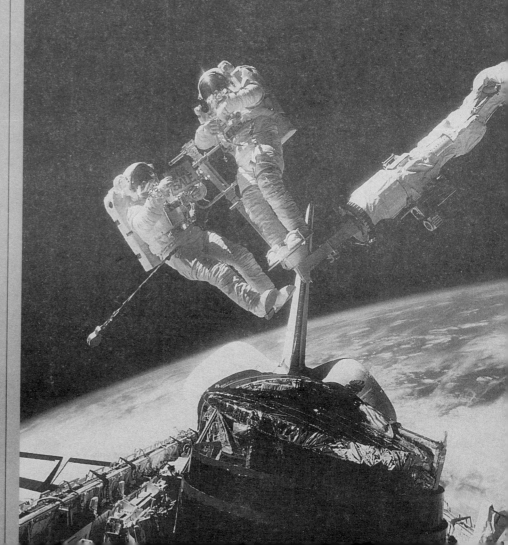

Genre	Comprehension Skills and Strategy	Text Features
Expository nonfiction	• Main Idea • Cause and Effect • Text Structure	• Captions • Diagrams • Labels

Scott Foresman Reading Street 2.1.2

PEARSON

Scott
Foresman

scottforesman.com

ISBN 0-328-13236-5

90000

9 780328 132362

Vocabulary

everywhere

live

machines

move

woman

work

world

Word count: 281

Note: The total word count includes words in the running text and headings only. Numerals and words in chapter titles, captions, labels, diagrams, charts, graphs, sidebars, and extra features are not included.

Think and Share

Read Together

1. What is the main idea of this book?
2. The author based this book on the problems of walking in space and the way astronauts solved them. Use the chart below to tell the problems and solutions you read about.

PROBLEM	SOLUTION

3. Find three nouns in the book that tell something about space walks. Use each in a sentence.
4. How do the pictures on pages 4 and 5 go together?

Astronauts build things in space. Astronauts took many space walks to build the International Space Station. Space walks in the future will help people everywhere. They will help every man, woman, and child better understand our world.

The International Space Station gives astronauts a place to live and work in space.

12

Space Walk

by Ginny Grissom

PEARSON

Scott Foresman

Editorial Offices: Glenview, Illinois • Parsippany, New Jersey • New York, New York
Sales Offices: Needham, Massachusetts • Duluth, Georgia • Glenview, Illinois
Coppell, Texas • Ontario, California • Mesa, Arizona

Every effort has been made to secure permission and provide appropriate credit for photographic material. The publisher deeply regrets any omission and pledges to correct errors called to its attention in subsequent editions.

Unless otherwise acknowledged, all photographs are the property of Scott Foresman, a division of Pearson Education.

Photo locators denoted as follows: Top (T), Center (C), Bottom (B), Left (L), Right (R), Background (Bkgd)

Cover: Bettmann/CORBIS; **1** CORBIS; **3** CORBIS; **4** Roger Ressmeyer/CORBIS; **5** CORBIS; **8** CORBIS; **9** Roger Ressmeyer/CORBIS; **10** CORBIS; **11** Bettmann/CORBIS

ISBN: 0-328-13236-5

2 3 4 5 6 7 8 9 10   V010   14 13 12 11 10 09 08 07 06 05

Astronauts take space walks to pick up objects. They bring them back to a spaceship. Sometimes they bring them back to Earth.

© Pearson Education, Inc.

Astronauts fix a broken satellite and put it back in orbit around Earth.

Space walks help astronauts solve problems in space.

Astronauts take space walks to fix broken machines.

What is a space walk?

When an astronaut goes outside a spaceship to work in space, that is a space walk.

In 1965, astronaut Ed White was the first American to walk in space.

Astronauts float in space. So they practice working underwater before they take a space walk. They do the same work underwater that they will do in space.

Astronaut Kathryn Thornton practiced for a space walk underwater.

In space, an astronaut's tools can float away.

These tools have loops. The astronaut can use the loops to tie the tools to the spacesuit.

Astronauts inspect their tools before bringing them into space.

In space, it is not easy to move around.

A special pack helps an astronaut move in space. The pack has rockets that help the astronaut move right, left, up, and down.

Today a spacesuit is like a small spaceship. The astronaut can steer in space.

There are problems for an astronaut on a space walk.

In space, there is no air to breathe. There is no water to drink. Rocks, ice, and "space junk" can hit you.

Astronaut Kathryn Thornton works on the Hubble Space Telescope in space.

A spacesuit helps with many of these problems. It has air, so the astronaut can breathe. It has water, so the astronaut can drink. The spacesuit protects the astronaut's whole body.

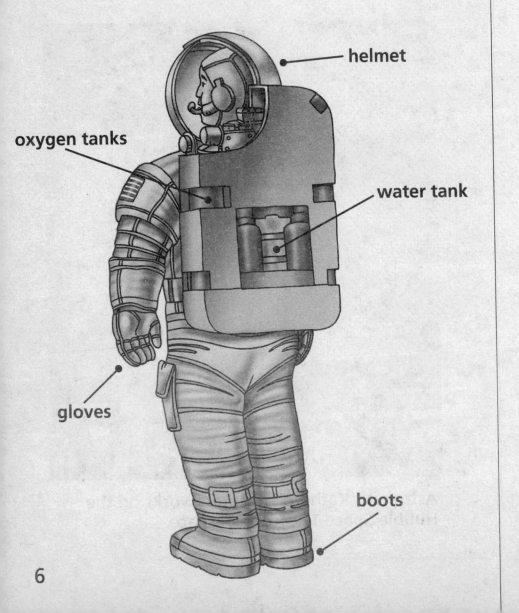

helmet

oxygen tanks

water tank

gloves

boots

Sometimes it is very hot in space. Other times it can be very cold.

A spacesuit has many tubes. They carry cold water. That keeps the astronaut cool.

Space gloves have heaters. They keep the astronaut's hands warm.

A spacesuit has many layers for protection.

Lexile,® and Reading Recovery™ are provided
in the Pearson Scott Foresman Leveling Guide.

Let's Camp at Crescent Lake

by C.A. Barnhart   illustrated by Mike Dammer

Genre	Comprehension Skills and Strategy
Realistic fiction	• Character and Setting • Sequence • Monitor and Fix Up

Scott Foresman Reading Street 2.1.3

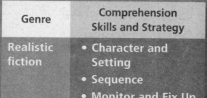

PEARSON

Scott
Foresman

scottforesman.com

Vocabulary

bear

build

couldn't

father

love

mother

straight

Word count: 262

Think and Share   (Read Together)

1. What is the setting at the beginning of the story? What is the setting at the end? How are they different?

2. What can you do if you are reading some dialogue but you are not sure who is speaking? Fill in the chart below. For each character, write down one thing he or she says in the story.

Character	What he or she says
Richard	
Jean	
Mother	
Father	

3. Sort the words in the list that have the blend *pl-* from the words with the blend *str-*. List: *explore, play, please, straight, plan, stream.*

4. On the last page of the story, Father asks a question. Reread the question. What do you think the answer should be? Why?

Animals in the Tide Pool

In this story, you read about visiting tide pools at the beach. Tide pools can be full of different kinds of small sea animals. This tide pool has round, green sea anemones and orange and purple starfish.

Different kinds of animals like to live in different kinds of places. Deer, chipmunks, and bears are often found in the mountains. Crabs, mussels, and seagulls are often found at the beach.

Tide pools are full of small, colorful sea animals, such as these starfish and anemones.

Let's Camp at Crescent Lake

by C.A. Barnhart
illustrated by Mike Dammer

PEARSON
Scott
Foresman

Editorial Offices: Glenview, Illinois • Parsippany, New Jersey • New York, New York
Sales Offices: Needham, Massachusetts • Duluth, Georgia • Glenview, Illinois
Coppell, Texas • Ontario, California • Mesa, Arizona

"This place is great!" Richard said.
"Hear the birds sing!" Mother said.
"See the tall trees!" Jean said.
"Smell the fresh air," Father said.
"Are you glad we came to Crescent Lake?"

11

Finally, it was time to go. Mother read the map. Father drove the car.

"Turn left here," Mother said. "Turn right there," she said. "Now straight down this road. We are almost there."

"Father has time off next week," Mother said. "Let's plan a trip."

"I'd love to camp at the beach," said Jean.

"Let's camp high on a mountain," said Richard.

"At the beach we could build a sand castle," said Jean. "We could float on the water. We could splash in the waves. We could even explore the tide pools."

4

Richard packed his own bag. He packed a warm sweater for the cold nights. He packed a swimsuit for the warm days.

9

Everyone helped. Mother found the tent. Father packed the food. Richard rolled up the sleeping bags. Jean folded the map.

"In the mountains we could sleep in a forest," said Richard. "We could fish in a stream. We could walk on a trail. We could even see a bear."

"I have an idea," Father said. "At Crescent Lake we can float on the water. We can walk on a trail. We can sleep in a a forest."

Richard and Jean said, "Please, let's camp at Crescent Lake!"

"Let's plan ahead," Mother said. "Make lists of things we'll need. First, write down *fresh water to drink*. Then write *food* and *tent* too."

Jean and Richard couldn't wait.

Science

Science

Earth Science

Genre	Comprehension Skills and Strategy	Text Features
Expository nonfiction	• Main Idea and Details • Author's Purpose • Text Structure	• Captions

Scott Foresman Reading Street 2.1.4

PEARSON
Scott
Foresman

scottforesman.com

ISBN 0-328-13242-X

90000

9 780328 132423

A Walk in the Mountains

by Kim Borland

Vocabulary

animals

early

eyes

full

warm

water

Word count: 373

Think and Share (Read Together)

1. What is this book about? Name two details that support your idea. Fill in a chart like the one below.

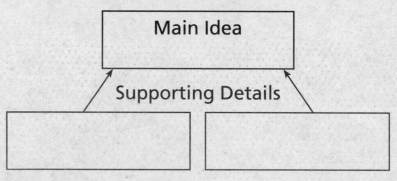

Main Idea

Supporting Details

2. Is this book fiction or nonfiction? What clues help you to know?

3. Here are three vocabulary words that are in this book: *full, warm, early.* Think of words that mean the opposite of these words. Use those opposite words in sentences.

4. Read again the first paragraph on page 9. What happens to a hare's fur when winter comes? How might that help the hare stay safe from its enemies?

We've had a full day of exploring. But there is more to see and learn about this special place. So the next time you see a mountain, think about all the interesting plants and animals that live there—from the bottom to the very top!

A Walk in the Mountains

by Kim Borland

PEARSON

Scott Foresman

Editorial Offices: Glenview, Illinois • Parsippany, New Jersey • New York, New York
Sales Offices: Needham, Massachusetts • Duluth, Georgia • Glenview, Illinois
Coppell, Texas • Ontario, California • Mesa, Arizona

All kinds of animals live in and around a mountain stream. Otters catch fish here. Deer and raccoons come for a drink.

Plants live near streams too. Their roots can find all the water they need.

Otters have webbed feet and are fast swimmers.

Raccoons are good climbers. They sometimes nest or hide in trees.

11

Look at this waterfall! The cold, clear water falls into a running stream below. The rushing water of a waterfall helps change the shape of a mountain. It slowly wears away the rock.

Yosemite National Park in California has the tallest waterfall in the United States.

It's early morning. The sun is just coming up. Everything is quiet on the mountain. But things are happening all around. All you have to do is keep your eyes and ears open. Let's take a walk and see what we can find.

The sun rises over the mountains.

3

Look up! Can you see the tops of the mountains? Some are sharp. Others are low and rounded.

These mountains are many, many years old.

The Appalachian Mountains are the oldest mountains in North America.

Did you see that? A hare just hopped across our path. Its fur is brown. But it will turn snow white when winter comes.

Hares feed on the leaves and grass that they find in the forests.

A hare's white coat protects it from other animals.

This hare is starting to turn white for winter.

The porcupine lives in these mountains all year long. It eats plants, twigs, and tree bark.

The golden eagle lives here too. It builds its nest way up high. But it flies down low to catch its food.

A golden eagle can glide for a long time without flapping its wings.

The porcupine has long sharp quills all over its body. They protect it from other animals.

Some mountains are so tall that their tops are covered in snow. It is very cold at the top. The place where the snow begins is called the *snow line*. Can you see the snow line on this mountain?

The highest peak in North America is Mount McKinley in Alaska.

Mountains are home to all kinds of plants and animals. Not many things live near the top. It is too cold. But it is warmer on the lower part of the mountain. There are many plants and animals.

Mountain goats are good climbers. They can jump from rock to rock on mountain slopes.

Grizzly bears can be found in the Rocky Mountains.

Trees, flowers, and other plants grow on the grassy hills. Insects live here too. Bees buzz all around. Butterflies fly from flower to flower.

Edelweiss is a type of mountain flower. It has hairy leaves. They help it hold water.

Edelweiss is a flower found in Europe, Asia, and South America.

Forests grow on the lower parts of mountains.

Suggested levels for Guided Reading, DRA,™
Lexile,® and Reading Recovery™ are provided
in the Pearson Scott Foresman Leveling Guide.

The Bear Man
A Native American Folk Tale

by Christine Wolf

Genre	Comprehension Skills and Strategy
Folk Tale	• Realism and Fantasy • Draw Conclusions • Monitor and Fix Up

Scott Foresman Reading Street 2.1.5

PEARSON

Scott
Foresman

scottforesman.com

ISBN 0-328-13245-4

9 780328 132454

90000

illustrated by
Sheila Bailey

Vocabulary

gone

learn

often

pieces

though

together

very

Word count: 358

Think and Share (Read Together)

1. Could this story have happened? Why or why not?

2. What do you think this story is trying to tell us? What is its message?

3. Copy the chart below. Write these words in the chart next to their meanings: *very, pieces, together*. Then use each word in a sentence.

Word	Meaning	Sentence
	much	
	parts of a whole	
	with one another	

4. What animal do you think you are most like? Why?

Today, the home of the Pawnee Nation is in Nebraska and Kansas. The Pawnee people have lived on wide-open lands for over 700 years.

The Pawnee call corn "the mother." They believe it is the most important thing they can grow.

The Pawnee have always hunted and farmed. They grew corn, squash, beans, and pumpkins.

The Pawnee warriors would make their hair stick up like horns. They used buffalo fat and paint on their faces and bodies.

Today, Pawnee Indians do many things. Some are doctors. Some are lawyers. Many work to help others in the Pawnee Nation.

The Bear Man
A Native American Folk Tale

by Christine Wolf
illustrated by Sheila Bailey

PEARSON
Scott
Foresman

Editorial Offices: Glenview, Illinois • Parsippany, New Jersey • New York, New York
Sales Offices: Needham, Massachusetts • Duluth, Georgia • Glenview, Illinois
Coppell, Texas • Ontario, California • Mesa, Arizona

ISBN: 0-328-13245-4

2 3 4 5 6 7 8 9 10 V010 14 13 12 11 10 09 08 07 06 05

The two bears told the Bear Man to be brave. They told him to be strong. The bears hugged him. Then they were gone.

The Bear Man made up a bear dance. To this day, the children still learn this dance.

The two bears fed the Bear Man. They made him well. Then they all went together to the Bear Man's home.

The Bear Man's family was very happy to learn he was alive.

This folk tale has been told by the Pawnee Indians for many years.

Once there was a young boy who was just like a bear. He walked like a bear. He hunted like a bear. He even slept like a bear.

His people thought they knew why he was like a bear.

Before the boy was born, his father was often away in the woods. One day he found a lost bear cub. It made him think of a child.

4

The bears cleaned him. They gave him water to drink. Then they lay down with the Bear Man. They warmed his cold body.

9

One day the Bear Man's people went to war. All the warriors were killed. Only the Bear Man lived. But he was badly hurt.

Two bears found him. One said, "I know him. He has played with us. He has shared his food with us. We must take care of him."

Though he was a great warrior, the boy's father was careful with the little bear. He talked to the bear. He gave him pieces of his own food. He even tied some of his own charms around the cub's neck.

"Someday," he told the cub, "I will have a child. If he is ever hurt, I hope he will be taken care of too."

Then the boy's father returned home. He told his wife about the cub. She thought about the little bear. She also thought about the baby she would have.

As the boy grew, he acted like a bear. He played with bears. He even said he could turn into a bear. He was known as the Bear Man.

And he became a great warrior, like his father.

Suggested levels for Guided Reading, DRA,
Lexile,® and Reading Recovery™ are provided
in the Pearson Scott Foresman Leveling Guide.

Social Studies   Social Studies

What to Do in an Emergency

by Christine Wolf

Genre	Comprehension Skills and Strategy	Text Features
Narrative nonfiction	• Sequence • Main Idea • Predict	• Captions • Headings • Lists

Scott Foresman Reading Street 2.2.1

PEARSON

Scott
Foresman

scottforesman.com

ISBN 0-328-13248-9

90000

9 780328 132485

Word count: 391

Think and Share (Read Together)

1. If you were in a house that was on fire, what would you do? Use a chart like the one below to list the steps in order.

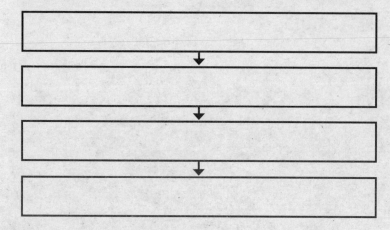

2. Imagine you are lost in a store. What do you think would happen once you tell an adult that you are lost?

3. Why is it important to listen when you are lost?

4. Why is it important to stay calm in an emergency?

What if *you* are in the accident?
Here are some tips:

- Stay calm and alert.
- Get out of danger.
- Check yourself for injuries.
- Call 9-1-1.

Remember: planning ahead can keep you safe!

Help prevent emergencies.
Always fasten your seatbelt.

12

What to Do in an Emergency

by Christine Wolf

PEARSON

Scott
Foresman

Editorial Offices: Glenview, Illinois • Parsippany, New Jersey • New York, New York
Sales Offices: Needham, Massachusetts • Duluth, Georgia • Glenview, Illinois
Coppell, Texas • Ontario, California • Mesa, Arizona

Opener ©Hutchings Stock Photography/Corbis; 1 Brand X Pictures/Getty Images; 3 ©Gabe Palmer/Corbis; 4 Brand X Pictures/Getty Images; 5 Getty Images; 6 PhotoEdit; 7 ©Royalty-Free/Corbis; 8 ©Hutchings Stock Photography/Corbis; 9 ©Charles O'Rear/ Corbis; 10 ©Ashley Cooper/Corbis; 11 ©Tim Wright/Corbis; 12 ©Royalty-Free/Corbis

ISBN: 0-328-13248-9

Copyright © Pearson Education, Inc.

2 3 4 5 6 7 8 9 10 V010 14 13 12 11 10 09 08 07 06 05

Do not try to move people who are hurt. The rescue team can do that. It is their job to pull people out of danger.

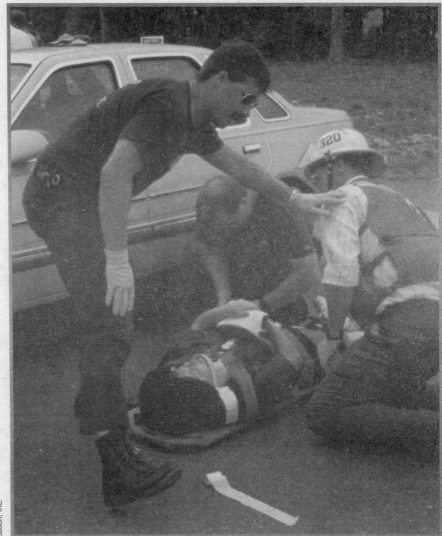

© Pearson Education, Inc.

Getting Help in an Accident

What if you see an accident, such as a car crash? The first thing to do is to call 9-1-1.

Tell the operator what you saw. Speak clearly, so you can be heard. Don't hang up until the operator tells you to.

Emergencies don't happen very often. But when they do, kids can help. You can take care of yourself and your family. Sometimes you can help others too.

Be Prepared

What would you do if you were lost? What if you were in a fire or an accident? This book will tell you how to plan ahead.

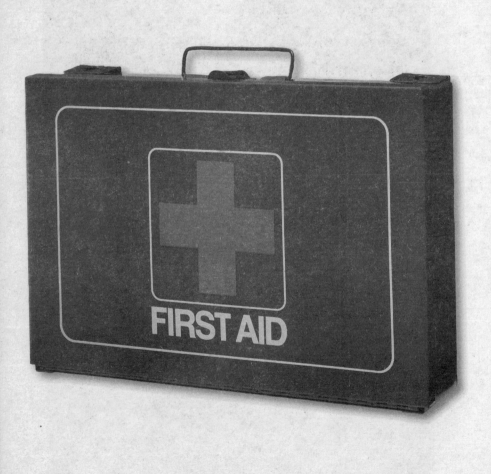

FIRST AID

Once you are out of danger, you can call 9-1-1.

Don't try to rescue a person or pet in a fire. That is the job of the firefighters.

Let the firefighters fight the fire.

Getting Out of a Fire

If you are in a house that is on fire, get out as fast as you can.

- Get down low. Smoke rises, so the air is easier to breathe closer to the floor.

- If your clothes are on fire, **stop, drop** to the ground, and **roll** to put the flames out.

- Break a window if it is the only way out.

- Don't stop to take anything with you.

Fire spreads quickly. Get to safety right away!

Here are some things you can do now to be ready for an emergency:

- Learn how to call 9-1-1 for help.

- Know your address and phone number.

- Make an emergency plan with your family.

- Know where there is a first-aid kit in your home.

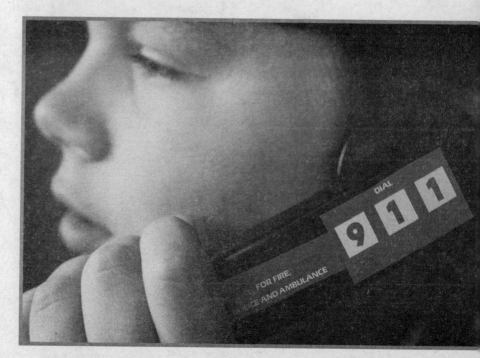

This boy knows how to call 9-1-1 for emergency help.

Getting Lost

Have you ever been lost? Know what to do when you are lost. That will help you stay calm. Here are some things to remember if it happens to you.

If You Are Indoors

- Go to the nearest counter or desk. Tell an adult you are lost.
- Know your address and phone number.

If You Are Outdoors

- Stay in the same spot.
- Listen for people calling your name.

Always stay close to the group if you are hiking outdoors.

Suggested levels for Guided Reading, DRA,
Lexile,® and Reading Recovery™ are provided
in the Pearson Scott Foresman Leveling Guide.

Genre	Comprehension Skills and Strategy
Animal fantasy	• Realism and Fantasy • Character, Setting, Plot • Prior Knowledge

Scott Foresman Reading Street 2.2.2

PEARSON

Scott
Foresman

scottforesman.com

ISBN 0-328-13251-9

90000

9 780328 132515

Warm and Fuzzy

by Kristin Cashore
illustrated by Rick Ewigleben

Vocabulary

certainly

either

great

laugh

second

worst

you're

Word count: 270

Think and Share

Read Together

1. Is this story real, or is it a fantasy? Why do you think so?

2. What did you know about knitting before you read this story? What did you learn about wool and knitting from the story?

3. Draw this chart on a separate sheet of paper. List all the contractions in this story. Then write the words that make up each contraction.

Contraction	Words

4. Why do you think the story is called *Warm and Fuzzy*?

When it is cold outside, you wear a warm coat and boots. You might also wear a scarf, a hat, and mittens or gloves.

When you grow out of your old winter clothes, what do you do with them? Well, here's an idea: Give them to people in need.

Many parts of our country are cold in winter, but not everyone can afford new coats or boots. Luckily, there are many places that collect clothing for people in need. If you have winter clothing to give, call a nearby thrift store. They will tell you what to do.

Give your old winter clothes to people who need them. Helping others can make you feel warm and fuzzy inside!

For Charity

12

Warm and Fuzzy

by Kristin Cashore
illustrated by Rick Ewigleben

PEARSON

Scott Foresman

Editorial Offices: Glenview, Illinois • Parsippany, New Jersey • New York, New York
Sales Offices: Needham, Massachusetts • Duluth, Georgia • Glenview, Illinois
Coppell, Texas • Ontario, California • Mesa, Arizona

"What a great scarf!" cried Geraldine. "Now my neck is warm and fuzzy!"

"And we are not too hot!" said Penny.

"Now let's call Great Aunt Mildred!" said Kenny. And so they did.

ISBN: 0-328-13251-9

At last, Kenny was done.
"Wow, Kenny," said Penny. "That's the longest scarf I've ever seen. Great Aunt Mildred would be proud."
"Let's find Geraldine!" yelled Jenny.

"You're certainly lucky to be a giraffe, Geraldine!" said Jenny. "Penny, Kenny, and I get too hot in our fuzzy wool!"
"Well, I think you're lucky to be sheep," said Geraldine. "My neck gets too cold!"

"Oh, dear," said Penny. "A cold neck must be the worst thing in the world!"

"I don't know," said Geraldine. "Hot fuzzy wool sounds pretty bad too."

4

Then Kenny began to knit. For seven days, he was either knitting or sleeping or eating.

"Who taught you how to knit?" asked Jenny.

"My Great Aunt Mildred," said Kenny.

9

Next, Penny spun the wool into yarn. "I'm glad you had this spinning wheel, Kenny," said Penny.

"It's from Great Aunt Mildred too," said Kenny.

Kenny sat up. "Friends," he said, "don't laugh. But I have an idea!"

"Oh, tell us!" they all cried. So Kenny told them his idea. And they thought it was a great one.

8

5

First, they cut Jenny's, Penny's, and Kenny's wool.

"I love your haircut, Kenny!" said Jenny.

"I'm so nice and cool now!" said Penny.

Second, Jenny brushed the wool with a big brush. "I'm glad you had this brush, Kenny," said Jenny.

"It was a gift from my Great Aunt Mildred," said Kenny. "She'll be glad we are using it."

Science

Science

Life Science

The Busy, Lively, Sleepy, and Quiet Pond

Genre	Comprehension Skills and Strategy	Text Features
Expository nonfiction	• Sequence • Cause and Effect • Summarize	• Captions • Labels

Scott Foresman Reading Street 2.2.3

PEARSON

Scott Foresman

scottforesman.com

ISBN 0-328-13254-3

9 780328 132546

90000

by Kim Borland   **illustrated by Bradley Clarke**

Vocabulary

above

ago

enough

toward

whole

word

Word count: 416

Think and Share (Read Together)

1. What do turtle babies do right after they hatch from their eggs?

2. Look at the drawings on page 12. In your own words, describe how the pond changes during the year. Begin with Spring.

3. Name an animal and a plant that live above the surface of the pond. Name an animal and a plant that live in or below the surface of the pond.

4. Imagine you are standing at the edge of the pond. What kinds of things could you see, hear, smell, feel, and taste? Make a chart like this one.

At the Pond

See	Hear	Smell	Feel	Taste

In a few months, it will be the spring again. The ice will melt, and the animals will return. Once again, the pond will be a busy, lively place!

Spring

Summer

Fall

Winter

The Busy, Lively, Sleepy, and Quiet Pond

by Kim Borland

illustrationed by Bradley Clarke

PEARSON

Scott Foresman

Editorial Offices: Glenview, Illinois • Parsippany, New Jersey • New York, New York
Sales Offices: Needham, Massachusetts • Duluth, Georgia • Glenview, Illinois
Coppell, Texas • Ontario, California • Mesa, Arizona

The cold winter winds blow. Snow drifts across the pond. Tracks show that some animals visit the pond in the winter.

What's the word for the pond in winter? Quiet.

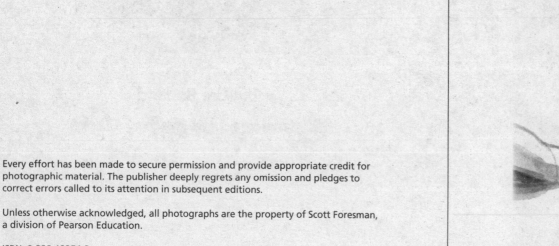

The winter days are cold. The ducks and geese are gone. The frogs and turtles sleep in the mud at the bottom of the pond.

The top of the pond turns to ice. Some animals live here all year long. They look for grass, seeds, and fruits around the pond.

The pond looks sleepy and quiet. Not much happens here. Or does it?

Take a closer look. Plants grow. Insects hum and buzz. Animals swim, fly, and hop. There is life near the water all year long. The pond is full of life! What's the word for the pond in spring? Busy!

Warm spring rain and melting snow fill the pond. Pond water is fresh, not salty like the ocean.

Trees begin to bud. Fruits and berries begin to grow. Flowers get a little taller every day.

The beavers work to repair their home, called a *lodge*. They add branches, logs, and mud to the lodge.

The beavers also gather food for the winter. They store food in the lodge and under the water. The beavers will have enough food for the whole winter.

© Pearson Education, Inc.

Beavers store tree bark, roots, shoots, and water plants underwater to last the winter.

In the spring, frogs and turtles dig out of their muddy winter homes on the bottom of the pond. The animals swim, eat, and lay eggs.

Ducks, geese, and birds build nests for their eggs. Soon the pond will be busy with animals and their young!

In the fall, the days grow cooler. The leaves on the trees change color. The ducks and geese fly away to warmer places. Turtles rest in the sun. Soon they will go deep under the mud at the bottom of the pond.

What's the word for the pond in fall? Sleepy!

Hot summer days warm the water. A mother duck and ducklings swim in the pond. They look under the water for food. Frogs sit on lily pads. They catch bugs with their long sticky tongues.

In the summer, the turtle eggs hatch. The baby turtles run toward the water.

The ducklings were born a few months ago. Now they learn to fly in circles above the pond.

What's the word for the pond in summer? Lively!

Genre	Comprehension Skills and Strategy
Realistic fiction	• Author's Purpose • Character, Setting, Plot • Story Structure

Scott Foresman Reading Street 2.2.4

PEARSON

Scott
Foresman

scottforesman.com

Jun and Pepper Grow Up

by Nancy Day

illustrations by Bob Masugals

Vocabulary

bought

people

pleasant

probably

scared

shall

sign

Word count: 362

Note: The total word count includes words in the running text and headings only. Numerals and words in chapter titles, captions, labels, diagrams, charts, graphs, sidebars, and extra features are not included.

Think and Share (Read Together)

1. Why do you think the author wrote *Jun and Pepper Grow Up*? Was it to share something that happened to the author, to teach the reader about something, or to tell an interesting story?

2. How did Jun feel about the puppy at the beginning of the story? How did Jun's feelings change by the end of the story?

3. Copy this chart on a separate sheet of paper. Write plural nouns from the story that end in *-s, -es,* and *-ies.* Write a sentence for each plural noun.

Ending	Noun	Sentence
-s		
-es		
-ies		

4. If you have a pet, tell how you help take care of it. If you don't have a pet, tell about a pet you would like to have.

Dogs grow up faster than people. Puppies become adult dogs in one or two years, but human babies become adults in 21 years. Some people like to think that one "dog year" is the same as seven or more human years.

But small dogs live longer than big dogs. So a small dog's "dog year" is the same as about four human years. Other things can affect how long a dog lives. Some kinds of dogs live longer than others.

Some dog experts say a three-month-old puppy is like a five-year-old child. At six months, the puppy is like a ten-year old. At one year, the dog is like a teenager. At two, a dog is a full-grown "adult."

Jun and Pepper Grow Up

by Nancy Day

illustrations by Bob Masugals

PEARSON

Scott Foresman

Editorial Offices: Glenview, Illinois • Parsippany, New Jersey • New York, New York
Sales Offices: Needham, Massachusetts • Duluth, Georgia • Glenview, Illinois
Coppell, Texas • Ontario, California • Mesa, Arizona

ISBN: 0-328-13257-8

"Remember how you used to be scared of Pepper?" Dad asked Jun.

Jun laughed. "He isn't a puppy anymore. He is a dog. I'm still a kid. But now I'm bigger. No matter how old we get, we will always be friends."

Pepper wagged his tail.

11

seven years old

two years old

One day Jun said, "Mom, Pepper keeps sneezing."

Pepper did not look happy. "Shall we take him to the vet?" Mom asked.

In her office, the vet pulled a bug out of Pepper's nose. Pepper wagged his tail.

five years old

eight years old

five weeks old

Dad came home with a box. "Look what I bought! Meet Pepper," he said. Mom said, "What a great surprise!" But Pepper ran over to Jun. The puppy jumped up. "No!" Jun cried. "Don't be a baby," said Soo Mi. "He is too big," said Jun.

Jun didn't like puppies jumping on him. He was still scared of dogs. Dad said, "It's okay. Soon you'll be bigger, and Pepper won't seem so scary."

"But so will Pepper!" said Jun. He wanted to be bigger than Pepper right now! Jun ran into the basement.

eight years old

twelve weeks old

five years old

Jun and Soo Mi played catch in the backyard. Pepper caught the ball. "Give it back!" Soo Mi yelled as she chased the dog all over the yard.

Pepper ran to Jun. He dropped the ball at Jun's feet. "Good dog!" said Jun.

eight years old

five years old

six months old

Jun learned to give Pepper his food and keep his water dish filled. The big puppy followed Jun everywhere. Now, Jun didn't mind so much. He even bought treats for Pepper.

five years old

eight years old

six months old

Jun didn't close the door. Pepper ran in after him. The puppy found Jun hiding behind the boxes. "No!" Jun shouted, "Don't jump."

Pepper just licked Jun's face. Jun was surprised. Pepper's tongue was pleasant. "This is probably a sign that you like me."

eight years old

six months old

five years old

When Jun went off to school, Mom took Pepper to dog school. Jun learned his ABCs. Pepper learned not to jump up on people.

In school, Jun learned to count to 100. Pepper learned how to go on walks.

Mom and Jun took Pepper for a walk. Jun held on to the leash. He counted all the way to 100 before Pepper pulled him off the sidewalk.

Social Studies

Giving Thanks Around the World

Genre	Comprehension Skills and Strategy	Text Features
Expository nonfiction	• Draw conclusions • Cause and Effect • Visualize	• Headings • Call Outs • Captions • Maps

Scott Foresman Reading Street 2.2.5

PEARSON

Scott
Foresman

scottforesman.com

ISBN 0-328-13260-8

90000

9 780328 132607

by Christine Wolf

Vocabulary

behind

brought

door

everybody

minute

promise

sorry

Word count: 350

Think and Share
Read Together

1. Why do you think round rice cakes are called "moon cakes" at the Chinese Moon Festival?

2. Read page 10 again. What words help you to see Thanksgiving in your mind?

3. Find the words in the book that have the long *a* sound spelled *a*, *ai*, and *ay*. List them in a chart like the one below.

Long *a* Words

a Words	*ai* Words	*ay* Words

4. What is your favorite holiday? Why? How do you celebrate? What do you do to help?

The national bird of the United States is the bald eagle. But in the 1700s, Benjamin Franklin wanted it to be the turkey instead.

The gobbling sounds wild turkeys make can be heard a mile away. The birds can fly up to 55 miles an hour. That's as fast as a car!

wild turkey

bald eagle

Benjamin Franklin liked the wild turkey better than the eagle.

Giving Thanks Around the World

by Christine Wolf

PEARSON
Scott Foresman

Editorial Offices: Glenview, Illinois • Parsippany, New Jersey • New York, New York
Sales Offices: Needham, Massachusetts • Duluth, Georgia • Glenview, Illinois
Coppell, Texas • Ontario, California • Mesa, Arizona

Giving Thanks in the United States

Our Thanksgiving is held in November. There are parades and football games. All day, wonderful smells come from behind kitchen doors. Kids count each minute as they wait until dinner. Then foods like turkey, sweet potatoes, and pies are brought out.

Thanksgiving Day parade

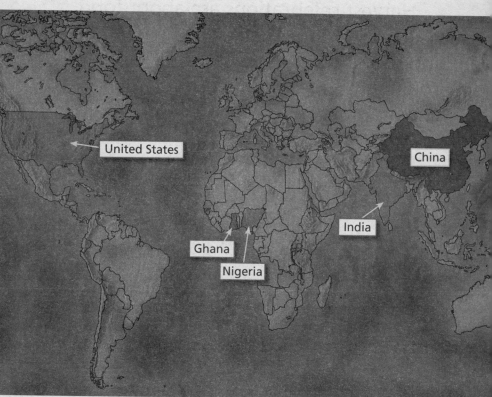

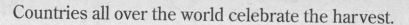

Countries all over the world celebrate the harvest.

Thanksgiving is a national holiday in the United States. If you love food, it's a great day!

Way back in 1621, the Pilgrims held a feast to celebrate their first harvest. This kind of celebration still takes place all over the world.

Harvest celebrations are about food. If you picture Thanksgiving, what do you see? Do you see a table full of food? You might see turkey, stuffing, and sweet potatoes, or yams.

Traditional clothes are often worn during celebrations in Africa.

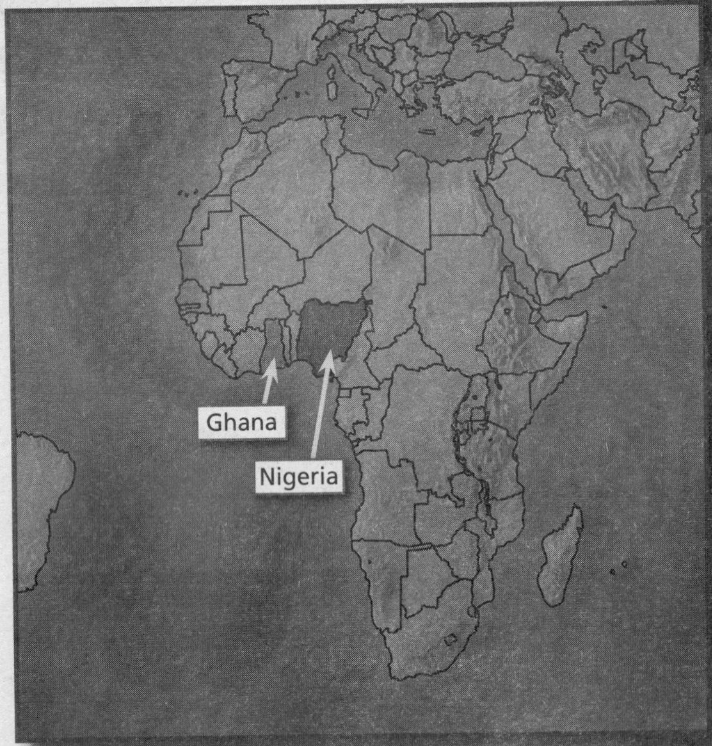

Ghana

Nigeria

People give thanks for the rain and the sun. They thank their cattle for helping in the rice fields. They decorate the cattle with flowers, bells, and colored rice powder.

© Pearson Education, Inc.

Giving Thanks in India

Villages in southern India celebrate the rice harvest with the Pongal Festival. The festival begins on January 13 and lasts for four days.

Villagers wear new clothes and visit family and friends. They eat a special sweet rice dish called *pongal.*

During the Pongal Festival, villagers use colored rice powder to make beautiful drawings on the ground.

India

Giving Thanks in Africa

African villages in Ghana and Nigeria have a whole celebration named after yams. Their Yam Festival is held in August. They give thanks for the first yam crop. Then, everybody gets to eat yams.

Giving Thanks in China

In China, people hold a harvest festival too. It is called the Moon Festival, or the Mid-Autumn Festival. It is held on the night of the full moon. To the Chinese, the moon is a symbol of good luck.

On that night, Chinese families gather outside to watch the moon. They have picnics and eat round rice cakes called moon cakes. There are also parades, puppet shows, and fireworks!

Moon cakes

China

In China, people celebrate the Moon Festival.

© Pearson Education, Inc.

6

Lexile® and Reading Recovery™ are provided
in the Pearson Scott Foresman Leveling Guide.

Genre	Comprehension Skills and Strategy
Realistic fiction	• Author's Purpose • Sequence • Story Structure

Scott Foresman Reading Street 2.3.1

PEARSON
Scott
Foresman

scottforesman.com

ISBN 0-328-13263-2

90000

9 780328 132638

Dotty's Dots

by Kama Einhorn
illustrated by Barb Dragony

Vocabulary

guess

pretty

science

shoe

village

watch

won

Word count: 296

Think and Share Read Together

1. What reason do you think the author had for writing this story?

2. This story begins in class. Where does it end and what happens in between? Use a chart like the one below to outline the events of the story.

Class:

↓

↓

↓

3. Have you ever won anything? Write two or three sentences about what you won or about why people like winning.

4. What clues are there on page 5 that Dotty's parents are interested in art?

Georges Seurat

In the story, Dotty says she likes the "dot artist" Seurat. Georges Seurat was born in Paris, France, in 1859. He began drawing while he was in school. The style of painting he created used tiny "points" or dots of paint. He thought that using color this way helped show how light changes what we see.

Dotty's Dots

by Kama Einhorn
illustrated by Barb Dragony

PEARSON

Scott
Foresman

Editorial Offices: Glenview, Illinois • Parsippany, New Jersey • New York, New York
Sales Offices: Needham, Massachusetts • Duluth, Georgia • Glenview, Illinois
Coppell, Texas • Ontario, California • Mesa, Arizona

ISBN: 0-328-13263-2

2 3 4 5 6 7 8 9 10 V010 14 13 12 11 10 09 08 07 06 05

"We always knew your name would come in handy someday!" Dotty's dad laughed.

© Pearson Education, Inc.

Then her mom came over. "*Dotty's Dots* won a blue ribbon," she said.

After science class, Dotty sat at her desk and listened to her teacher, Mr. Dean, talk about a school art show. Each student could enter one piece of art.

Dotty started to think. Bill said he'd draw his team playing soccer. Dotty told Maria that she should enter her pretty, clay turtle. But sadly, Dotty had no idea for her own art.

At home, Dotty worried. She couldn't even guess what she would create.

Her mom said, "How about painting an apple tree?"

Her dad asked, "Can you draw using your name?"

At the school art show Dotty drank punch and looked at her friends' art. Jean had painted a real wagon wheel in all different colors. Dan had drawn one of his dreams.

Dotty liked to watch everyone look at her dots.

Finally, she finished. There was a little dot village, little dot bees and fleas, and little dot people eating dot peas. The people even wore little dot shoes.

"It's pretty," Dotty thought. "I'll call it *Dotty's Dots.*"

"What do you mean?" asked Dotty.

"Do you remember when we went to the art show?" asked dad.

Mom added, "Remember the painter you called the dot artist?"

"Seurat. I liked him a lot! I think I said that over and over. Yes, I remember!" laughed Dotty.

"Start drawing dots, Dotty," Dad said.

Dotty liked the idea. She knew she could do it.

Dotty took crayons, markers, and a giant piece of paper, and started dotting away. She made big dots, little dots, and dots of every color. She filled her paper with thousands of dots. It took all week.

Social Studies

Social Studies

Mina's Day

by Kim Borland

Genre	Comprehension Skills and Strategy	Text Features
Narrative nonfiction	• Draw Conclusions • Fact and Opinion • Visualize	• Captions • Map

Scott Foresman Reading Street 2.3.2

PEARSON

Scott
Foresman

scottforesman.com

ISBN 0-328-13266-7

90000

9 780328 132669

Vocabulary

answer

company

faraway

parents

picture

school

wash

Word count: 292

Think and Share (Read Together)

1. What important news might a school principal share with children at the morning meeting?

2. Describe the New Year's kite flying celebration. What would your kite look like?

3. Use the word rating chart below to rate these words: *calm, rainy, neighborhood, important, bow.*

Word	Know	Have Seen	Don't Know
calm			
rainy			
neighborhood			
important			
bow			

4. How is Mina's life the same as yours? How is it different?

Kite flying is my favorite part of the celebration. We all make wishes for the new year as the kites float high into the air.

Traditional Korean kites are shaped like rectangles. Many have colorful drawings.

Mina's Day

by Kim Borland

PEARSON

Scott Foresman

Editorial Offices: Glenview, Illinois • Parsippany, New Jersey • New York, New York
Sales Offices: Needham, Massachusetts • Duluth, Georgia • Glenview, Illinois
Coppell, Texas • Ontario, California • Mesa, Arizona

Every effort has been made to secure permission and provide appropriate credit for photographic material. The publisher deeply regrets any omission and pledges to correct errors called to its attention in subsequent editions.

Unless otherwise acknowledged, all photographs are the property of Scott Foresman, a division of Pearson Education.

Photo locators denoted as follows: Top (T), Center (C), Bottom (B), Left (L), Right (R), Background (Bkgd)

Opener (TL) ©Charles & Josette Lenars/Corbis; Opener (BR) ©Paul Hurd/Stone/Getty Images; 1 ©Michael S. Yamashita/Corbis; 3 ©Charles & Josette Lenars/Corbis; 4 ©Jose Fuste Raga/Corbis; 6 Getty Images; 7 ©Paul Hurd/Stone/Getty Images; 8 ©Michael S. Yamashita/Corbis; 9 ©Bohemian Nomad Picturemakers/Corbis; 10 ©Michael S. Yamashita/Corbis; 11 ©Chung Sung-Jun/Getty Images; 12 ©Ronnie Kaufman/Corbis

ISBN: 0-328-13266-7

Copyright © Pearson Education, Inc.

One of the most important holidays in Korea is New Year's Day.
We visit with friends and family. We make kites together.

Making and flying kites are traditional parts of the Korean New Year's celebration.

© Pearson Education, Inc.

On weekends, the palace is filled with people. Many come from faraway places.

Many visitors want to take a picture before they go.

Long ago, the Palace of Shining Happiness was made up of 500 buildings!

Hello! My name is Mina. I am seven years old.

I live in South Korea. My home is in a large city called Seoul.

Korea is made up of two countries: North Korea and South Korea.

I like living in Seoul. Some things here are old and some things are new. In Seoul, there are tall, shiny, new buildings. There are also buildings from long ago.

I would love to show you the Palace of Shining Happiness. I think it is the most beautiful place anywhere! People visit all the time to learn about the kings and queens of long ago.

The palace was once the home of the royal family.

4

9

After school, students stay and help clean. We empty trash cans, sweep the floors, and wash the blackboards.

Korean children go to school on Saturday morning too.

The summers are very hot. The winters are long and cold. We call June, July, and August the rainy season. Why? The answer is that sometimes it rains almost every day for a month!

I live with my parents, my two brothers, and my baby sister.

My family and I like to play games together. Our favorite game is *yut*. You throw sticks into the air.

Your score depends on which way your sticks land.

In the game of *yut*, each stick has a smooth side and a rough side.

My friends and I often walk to school together. We keep one another company on the long walk.

At the morning meeting, the principal shares important news with everyone. Then children bow, thank the principal, and go off to class.

When we get to school, we go to the playground. There we have a morning meeting.

6

7

Science

Science

Life Science

Insect or Arachnid?

Genre	Comprehension Skills and Strategy	Text Features
Expository nonfiction	• Cause and Effect • Main Idea • Monitor and Fix Up	• Captions • Labels • Callouts

Scott Foresman Reading Street 2.3.3

ISBN 0-328-13269-1

90000

9 780328 132690

by Kristin Cashore

Vocabulary

been

believe

caught

finally

today

tomorrow

whatever

Word count: 284

Think and Share   Read Together

1. How does a ladybug protect itself? Why does it need to protect itself?

2. Think about what you have learned about insects and arachnids. Use a diagram like the one below to show how they are the same and how they are different.

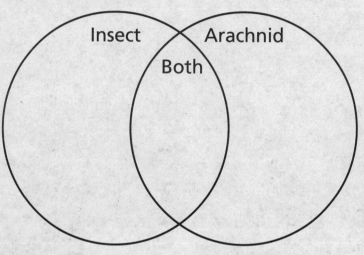

3. On a separate sheet of paper, write all the compound words from this book. What small words make up these compound words?

4. Do you enjoy studying insects and arachnids? Why or why not?

Insects and arachnids have always been easy to mix up. You will not mix them up anymore!

If you see a bug today or tomorrow, count its legs. Count the parts of its body. Check for antennae. Check for wings. Now will you know which it is—insect or arachnid?

Insect or Arachnid?

by Kristin Cashore

PEARSON

Scott Foresman

Editorial Offices: Glenview, Illinois • Parsippany, New Jersey • New York, New York
Sales Offices: Needham, Massachusetts • Duluth, Georgia • Glenview, Illinois
Coppell, Texas • Ontario, California • Mesa, Arizona

ISBN: 0-328-13269-1

Many scorpions live in the desert.

Scorpions can be eight inches long.

Scorpions keep themselves safe in a special way. They have poison in their tails! If a scorpion is attacked, it will sting. Whatever you do, do not pick one up!

A tick is an arachnid.

A mite is an arachnid.

Finally, a scorpion is the biggest arachnid!

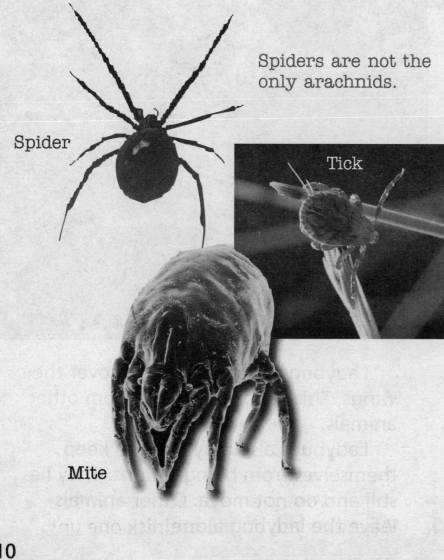

Spiders are not the only arachnids.

Spider

Tick

Mite

Many people believe that all bugs and creepy crawly things are insects. This is not true!
A spider is not an insect. It is an arachnid.
What is the difference?

There are thousands of types of insects and arachnids.

Insects

All insects have six legs. An ant has six legs.

All insects have a body in three parts. An ant has a body in three parts.

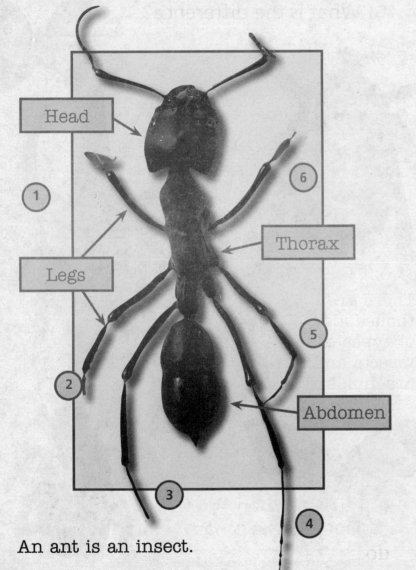

Head

Legs

Thorax

Abdomen

1

2

3

4

5

6

An ant is an insect.

A ladybug hides its wings under its red shell.

Ladybugs have a hard shell over their wings. This keeps them safe from other animals.

Ladybugs also play dead to keep themselves from being caught. They lie still and do not move. Other animals leave the ladybug alone!

A dragonfly is an insect.

A grasshopper is an insect.

A butterfly is an insect.

Finally, a ladybug is an insect.

Butterfly

Dragonfly

Grasshopper

Look for legs. Look for wings. Look for antennae. Are these insects?

A fly is an insect.

Wings

Abdomen

Thorax

Head

Legs

Antennae

All insects have antennae. Antennae are found on an insect's head. Insects use them to feel and smell.

Not all insects have wings, but many do.

Arachnids

An arachnid can be tiny, just like an insect. Arachnids and insects are different, though.

All arachnids have eight legs, not six. An arachnid's body is in two parts, not three.

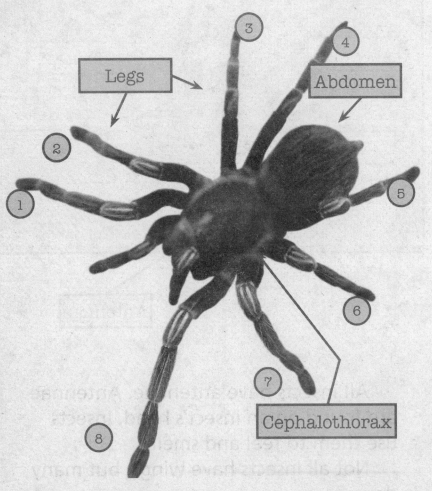

Legs

Abdomen

Cephalothorax

A spider is an arachnid.

Arachnids never have antennae.
Arachnids never have wings.

Spiders spin beautiful webs with their own silk.

Lexile,® and Reading Recovery™ are provided
in the Pearson Scott Foresman Leveling Guide.

An International Food Fair!

by Jana Martin

illustrations by Joe Bucco

Genre	Comprehension Skills and Strategy
Realistic fiction	• Theme and Plot • Compare and Contrast • Predict

Scott Foresman Reading Street 2.3.4

PEARSON
Scott
Foresman

scottforesman.com

ISBN 0-328-13272-1

Vocabulary

alone

buy

daughters

half

many

their

youngest

Word count: 381

Think and Share (Read Together)

1. What was the theme, or "big idea," of this story?

2. Do you think the Kyles will try foods from other countries again? What clues helped you predict what they might do?

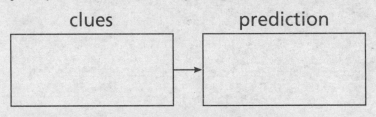

clues   prediction

3. How did the Kyles introduce their children? Which of the children was born last?

4. Which foods in the story do you think you would like to try? Why?

The pancakes that wrapped the Chinese spring rolls would have been made from rice. The pancakes known as French crepes would have been made from wheat. If you were to go to Mexico, you would find something that looks like a pancake that is made from corn—a tortilla.

Different countries use different grains to make their dough, but the foods often end up with similar shapes. This is because people worldwide have similar needs. Think about foods you know that are easy to cook or easy to carry.

Many countries have some kind of pancake. In the United States, pancakes usually come with butter and syrup.

12

An International Food Fair!

by Jana Martin

illustrations by Joe Bucco

PEARSON

Scott Foresman

Editorial Offices: Glenview, Illinois • Parsippany, New Jersey • New York, New York
Sales Offices: Needham, Massachusetts • Duluth, Georgia • Glenview, Illinois
Coppell, Texas • Ontario, California • Mesa, Arizona

12 ©Mark McLane/Stone/Getty Images

ISBN: 0-328-13272-1

"Hey," Amy said. "Know what? That was the best dinner ever."

"I'm glad we forgot whose turn it was to cook!" said Mrs. Kyle. "It was fun to eat dinner around the world!"

The Kyles had their dinner. Now it was time for dessert.

Mr. Kyle laughed as Danny eyed the table with food from Italy. "Would you like a cannoli?" Mr. Kyle asked. "It's stuffed with sweet cheese and chocolate chips."

"Yummy!" said Amy, Allie, and Danny, together.

Who was supposed to make dinner at the Kyles' house tonight?

"Isn't it your turn?" Mrs. Kyle said to Mr. Kyle.

"I thought it was your turn," Mr. Kyle said to Mrs. Kyle. "What should we do?"

Mr. and Mrs. Kyle taught at the local college. Their children, Amy, Allie, and Danny loved to visit the college. They liked the fact that the students came from around the world.

"Hey," Mr. Kyle said. "Let's not eat alone. Tonight is the college's International Food Fair. We can buy food from other countries!"

4

Next, the Kyles decided to try food from France. The French girl said, "Try some *crepes*. They are very thin pancakes."

She poured batter on a hot pan, then added cheese. "Who wants a bite?" she asked, folding the cooked crepe. Everyone did!

© Pearson Education, Inc.

9

"Welcome to a tiny slice of Ghana," said the boys at another table.

"Ghana's in West Africa," Amy said. "I learned that in school. What's the mushy stuff?"

The boys laughed. "That is mashed yam, called *fufu*. It's like bread to us."

Fufu

GHANA

8

The food fair took up half of the gym! There were tables and flags. Students and teachers offered food from their homes. There were people from Mexico, Thailand, France, Kenya, and many other countries.

MEXICO

JAPAN

INDIA

5

"Hello Mr. and Mrs. Kyle!" said a girl at the Chinese food table. "These must be your children."

"These are our daughters, Amy and Allie," Mrs. Kyle said. "And this is our son, Danny. He is our youngest."

"What are you serving?" asked Mr. Kyle.

"*Dim sum*," said the girl. "The words mean 'touch the heart,' but it really just means 'snack.' Many dishes are a part of dim sum, like the spring roll. It's a thin pancake that is rolled around pork and vegetables, then fried."

"Delicious!" said Danny, taking two.

TEA

shu Mai

flower Rolls

Spring Rolls

CHINESE DIM SUM

Social Studies

Biography

Thomas Adams Invents Chewing Gum

by Jessica Quilty

Genre	Comprehension Skills and Strategy	Text Features
Biography	• Cause and Effect • Draw Conclusions • Monitor and Fix Up	• Captions • Illustrations • Time Line

Scott Foresman Reading Street 2.3.5

PEARSON

Scott
Foresman

scottforesman.com

ISBN 0-328-13275-6

90000

9 780328 132751

illustrated by Ralph Canaday

Vocabulary

clothes

hours

money

neighbor

only

question

taught

Word count: 417

Think and Share Read Together

1. Thomas Adams was sad and felt like throwing his chicle in the river. What was the cause of this? Use a chart like the one below to show the relationship between cause and effect.

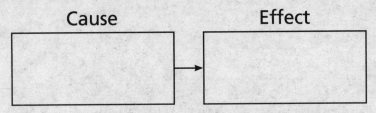

Cause		Effect
	→	

2. What information in the caption on page 5 might help you understand why Santa Anna would know about trees in Mexico?

3. On page 8, we read that Adams saw a neighbor at the drugstore. How does this help us guess that Adams was near his home?

4. Look at the time line on page 12. Before Adams' invention, there was only wax gum. What happened after Adams' New York Gum No. 1 was made?

Thomas Adams stopped working when he was 81 years old. His sons took over Adams and Sons.

Today we have many kinds of chewing gum to choose from, but it all started with Thomas Adams and one little girl buying wax gum. You never know where you might find the idea for a great invention.

GUM TIME LINE

Curtis White Mountain Wax Gum 1850

Adams' New York Gum No. 1 1870

Dentyne Gum 1899

Wrigley's Doublemint Gum 1914

Dubble Bubble Bubble Gum 1928

| 1850s | 1860s | 1870s | 1880s | 1890s | 1900s | 1910s | 1920s |

Thomas Adams Invents Chewing Gum

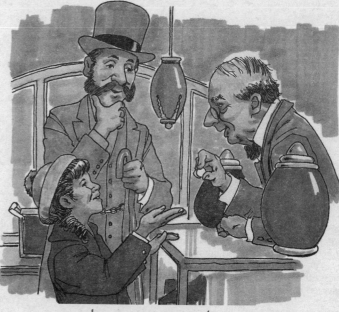

by Jessica Quilty
illustrated by Ralph Canaday

PEARSON
Scott Foresman

Editorial Offices: Glenview, Illinois • Parsippany, New Jersey • New York, New York
Sales Offices: Needham, Massachusetts • Duluth, Georgia • Glenview, Illinois
Coppell, Texas • Ontario, California • Mesa, Arizona

Adams invented a machine to sell his gum. Then he started a company called Adams and Sons. He traveled across the United States to sell his gum. He sold a lot of gum, so he made a lot of money.

ISBN: 0-328-13275-7

© Pearson Education, Inc.

Adams invented a machine to make his gum. He started with only one kind of gum. He named his gum *Adams' New York Gum No. 1.* Next, he made flavored gums. He made a licorice gum and a fruit gum.

Machines such as this one were used to make Adams' gum in the early 1900s.

Have you ever wondered about chewing gum? Gum has a long history. Long ago, Native Americans made gum from tree sap. Later, gum was made from wax. Thomas Adams invented the kind of gum we chew today.

Spruce tree sap was once used to make chewing gum.

Thomas Adams was born in New York in 1818. He was an inventor. Adams invented a new way to feed horses. He invented a new way to light lamps. His best invention was a new way to make chewing gum. Where did his gum idea come from?

Adams had been chewing chicle as he worked on the tires. It was much better than wax gum. Adams made the chicle into small sticks that he could wrap and sell. He sold his chicle gum at drugstores.

Adams knew that people in Mexico chewed chicle.

Later, Adams went to the drugstore. Adams's neighbor, a little girl, was buying wax gum. Adams got a new idea. He asked the storeowner a question.

"Would you sell a new kind of chewing gum?" Adams asked.

"Nothing would make me happier," the storeowner said.

Adams met a man named Antonio Lopez de Santa Anna. Santa Anna taught Adams about chicle, the rubbery sap of a tree that grows in Mexico. Santa Anna thought that Adams could mix chicle with rubber to make cheaper buggy tires.

Antonio Lopez de Santa Anna, the ex-president of Mexico, taught Adams about chicle.

Adams liked Santa Anna's idea. He bought one ton of chicle from Mexico. He shipped it by boat from Mexico to his home in New York.

Chicle comes from sapodilla trees that grow in Mexico. It is a lot like rubber.

6

Adams worked for hours every day. His clothes got dirty. He wanted to sell the chicle tires and make a lot of money.

The idea for tires did not work because chicle melted in the heat. Adams was sad. He felt like throwing the chicle in the river.

7

Social Studies

Social Studies

Quilting Memories

by Jiang Qingling

Genre	Comprehension Skills and Strategy	Text Features
Expository nonfiction	• Compare and Contrast • Main Idea • Text Structure	• Captions • Headings

Scott Foresman Reading Street 2.4.1

PEARSON

Scott Foresman

scottforesman.com

ISBN 0-328-13278-0

9 780328 132782

90000

Vocabulary

blankets

quilt

pretended

stuffing

trunks

unpacked

wrapped

Word count: 471

Reader Response

1. Compare the friendship block quilt to Diane Gaudynski's "Sweetheart on Parade" quilt. In what ways are the quilts similar? How are they different? Use a Venn diagram like the one shown below to record your ideas.

    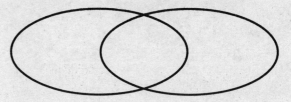

2. This book told about a few ways to preserve important memories. What did it tell about first, next, and last?

3. If something is *valuable* it means that it is very special to someone. What do you have that is *valuable* to you?

4. How did you know what page 6 of this book was going to be about before you read the whole page?

Preserving the Past

People have many ways of saving valuable memories. Some people try to save knowledge about historical events. Other people create objects to remember personal events.

There are many ways to preserve the past. Writing down events and quilting are just a few. Can you think of any other ways?

Collage of family photos

Quilting Memories

by Jiang Qingling

PEARSON

Scott Foresman

Editorial Offices: Glenview, Illinois • Parsippany, New Jersey • New York, New York
Sales Offices: Needham, Massachusetts • Duluth, Georgia • Glenview, Illinois
Coppell, Texas • Ontario, California • Mesa, Arizona

Hillary was very sick. Diane said that if Hillary got better, Diane would make a special quilt just for her. Diane kept her promise. She made a beautiful green-and-rose-colored quilt for Hillary. She got the idea because she noticed cats love to lie on quilts.

"Sweetheart on Parade" was created for Hillary the cat by Diane Gaudynski.

Photo locators denoted as follows: Top (T), Center (C), Bottom (B), Left (L), Right (R), Background (Bkgd)

Opener: (R) ©DK Images, (Bkgd) Getty Royalty Free, 1 ©DK Images; 4 ©DK Images; 5 ©DK Images; 6 Library of Congress; 7 Library of Congress; 10 The Museum of the American Quilters' Society; 11 Diane Gaudynski's quilt "Sweathearts on Parade"

ISBN: 0-328-13278-0

Copyright © Pearson Education, Inc.

2 3 4 5 6 7 8 9 10 V010 14 13 12 11 10 09 08 07 06 05

The "Cat" Quilt

A woman named Diane Gaudynski has made many quilts. Some of her quilts have been put on display. Some have won quilting awards. She once made a quilt for her cat, Hillary.

Many quilts are displayed in the Museum of the American Quilters' Society in Paducah, Kentucky.

Have you ever looked through a family photo album? Photos may help you remember events. They may also help you catch the mood of the moment. Did you know that there are many ways to create and capture memories without using a camera?

Scrapbooks, Journals, and Stories

People can save memories by making scrapbooks. Scrapbooks are blank books. They can be filled with pictures, papers, and other items. They make it easy to see what happened in the past.

Some people keep journals. In a journal or a diary, people write down their memories.

People made the blocks at the same time. They had a party to make the quilt. All of the blocks were sewn together. Then the quilt was given as a wedding gift.

Making a friendship block quilt isn't easy. It takes a long time. But the finished quilt reminds people of special memories.

Remembering Friends

This is a friendship block quilt. Many people worked together to make this quilt. Can you count how many blocks there are? Each block was made by a different person, and each block has the quilter's name in it.

There are ninety blocks in this quilt. What can you tell about each block?

Some people like to share their thoughts by telling stories. People can relive their past when they share stories.

Have your parents or grandparents ever told you a story about their childhood? Maybe they pretended to be young again? Stories teach us about the past.

Quilts

Making quilts is another way people remember the past. You may have wrapped yourself in a quilt to keep warm. But some people make quilts as a way to remember the past. Quilts can be decorated with symbols of special times and works of art.

This is a "kimono quilt" created by Japanese American quilter Yuki Sugiyama.

Quilts can be large or small. Sometimes, stuffing is used to make quilts thicker. Many quilts are made with bright colors and fine details. Some very old quilts hang on walls in museums. Other quilts are used as special family blankets.

Quilts may be stored in trunks. The quilts can be unpacked when they are ready to be displayed.

Science

Science

Life Science

It's Alive!

by Linda Yoshizawa

Genre	Comprehension Skills and Strategy	Text Features
Expository nonfiction	• Fact and Opinion • Cause and Effect • Ask Questions	• Headings • Captions • Labels

Scott Foresman Reading Street 2.4.2

PEARSON
Scott
Foresman

scottforesman.com

ISBN 0-328-13281-0

9 780328 132812

90000

Word count: 432

Reader Response

1. Is it a fact or an opinion on page 7 that a cactus can live for a long time with a little bit of water? How can you tell?

2. Make up a short quiz about what you have read. Write two questions and their answers.

Questions	Answers

3. On page 3 you learned that some plants have *fruit.* Which page in this book shows a picture of a plant with fruit?

4. How did the caption and picture on page 3 add to what you learned on this page?

When plants get what they need, they grow healthy and strong. When plants are healthy and strong, our environment is a better place.

We know plants are at work when we harvest apples from a tree or grapes from a vine. We also know plants are at work when we breathe fresh, clean air.

Fruit and flowers may grow on trees, bushes, or vines.

12

It's Alive!

by Linda Yoshizawa

PEARSON
Scott Foresman

Editorial Offices: Glenview, Illinois • Parsippany, New Jersey • New York, New York
Sales Offices: Needham, Massachusetts • Duluth, Georgia • Glenview, Illinois
Coppell, Texas • Ontario, California • Mesa, Arizona

Plants and animals share the air around them. They use air in different ways.

Animals breathe in oxygen. They breathe out carbon dioxide. Plants take in carbon dioxide and give off oxygen. In this way, they both need each other.

Plants help keep the air clean for people and animals.

© Pearson Education, Inc.

Unless otherwise acknowledged, all photographs are the property of Scott Foresman, a division of Pearson Education.

Photo locators denoted as follows: Top (T), Center (C), Bottom (B), Left (L), Right (R), Background (Bkgd)

Opener: Corbis Royalty; 1 Digital Vision; 3 DK Images; 4 Corbis Royalty, Digital Vision, Brand X Pictures; 5 Brand X Pictures; 6 Corbis Royalty; 7 Digital Vision; 9 Corbis Royalty; 10 Corbis Royalty; 12 Digital Vision

ISBN: 0-328-13281-0

2 3 4 5 6 7 8 9 10 V010 14 13 12 11 10 09 08 07 06 05

Plants Need Air

Plants need water and sunlight to survive. They need one more thing too. Like all living things, plants need air.

Air is made up of many different gases. One of those gases is carbon dioxide. Plants take carbon dioxide from the air. Along with water, nutrients, and light, they use it to make food.

So Many Plants

There are all kinds of plants. Some are big, and some are small. Some grow tall on strong stems. Some are vines that climb up walls and fences. Some plants have fruit. Some have smooth stems and leaves. Some have hard, bumpy bark.

Some redwood trees grow to be 350 feet tall. That's taller than the Statue of Liberty.

All plants are different, but they are alike in some ways too. Big or small, they are all living things. They grow and they change. Some large plants start out as tiny seeds. When they get what they need, they grow into large plants.

Corn kernels are seeds that grow into tall stalks.

Some plants need a lot of light. Some only need a little. If plants cannot get the light they need, they will not be healthy. They may even die.

This daisy got very little light. It died.

Plants Need Light

Plants need more than nutrients and water to grow. They also need light. Plants use the sunlight that falls on their leaves to make food.

This daisy gets a lot of light. It is healthy.

Plants grow almost everywhere. You can find plants in warm and cold climates. They can grow wherever they get the things they need. Plants need water, light, and air to live.

Crocus in the snow

8

5

Plants Need Water

Water dissolves nutrients from the soil so plants can use them. Nutrients are what living things need to grow and have energy.

The stem of a plant is filled with tiny tubes. The tubes carry water from the roots to the leaves. The leaves use the nutrients in the water to make food.

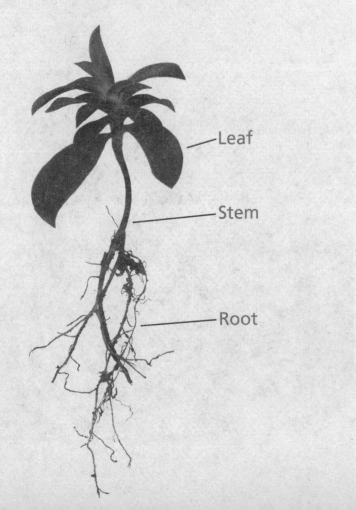

—Leaf

—Stem

—Root

Even plants that grow in dry desert climates need water. Deserts do not get much rain. Desert plants have adapted to dry climates. For example, a cactus can store water in its stem. A cactus can live for a long time on a little bit of water.

Cactus

Suggested levels for Guided Reading, DRA,™
Lexile,® and Reading Recovery™ are provided
in the Pearson Scott Foresman Leveling Guide.

Genre	Comprehension Skills and Strategy
Animal fantasy	• Compare and Contrast • Setting • Graphic Organizers

Scott Foresman Reading Street 2.4.3

PEARSON

Scott
Foresman

scottforesman.com

ISBN 0-328-13284-5

9 780328 132843

90000

Frog Friends

by Megan Litwin

illustrated by Sheila Bailey

Reader Response

1. How are Danny and Fred alike? How are they different?

2. Using a chart like the one below, write about what happened in the beginning, the middle, and the end of the story.

Beginning	Middle	End

3. Find three words in this book that end with *-ful*. Write down the words, and then use each one in a complete sentence.

4. What does Fred mean when he says on page 11, "We all have something that makes us special"?

Frogs

Frogs are amphibians. This means they live part of their life in water and part on land. Frogs begin life as tadpoles in the water. They breathe through gills like fish. The tadpoles grow into frogs. They lose their tail and gills, and they grow legs and lungs. Now they are adult frogs that live and breathe on land.

Like all living things, frogs need air, food, and water to live. They eat insects, worms, and snails. Frogs also shed their skin as they grow. Then they eat it!

Bullfrog tadpole

Frog Friends

by Megan Litwin
illustrated by Sheila Bailey

PEARSON
Scott Foresman

Editorial Offices: Glenview, Illinois • Parsippany, New Jersey • New York, New York
Sales Offices: Needham, Massachusetts • Duluth, Georgia • Glenview, Illinois
Coppell, Texas • Ontario, California • Mesa, Arizona

"Thanks, Danny," Fred said.
"You're welcome, Fred," Danny said.
"Can you show me that jump again? I wish I could jump that far. My legs aren't as strong as your legs."
"We all have something that makes us special, don't we?" Fred smiled.

Fred leapt forward at once. He disappeared safely into the deep pond just as a large bird tried to grab him. The bird flew away. Danny sat very still in his tree.

It was a beautiful summer day at the pond. Danny, a green tree frog, was enjoying the sounds of summer from his perch atop a tall tree. Down in the pond below, his friend Fred, a bullfrog, sat near the water. Fred was waiting for his lunch.

Just then a fly crawled near Fred.
Fred's long, sticky tongue shot out in a
flash and caught the tiny insect.

"Delicious! I'm full now," he said
loudly. He had already eaten three other
insects and a worm in the past hour.

Fred sat by the pond and felt bad
about what he had said. Danny was
always excited about everything. It was
what Fred liked most about him.

Just as Fred was about to apologize,
he felt a cold shadow fall over him. Then
he heard Danny's warning call.

4

9

As Danny kept talking about his day, Fred felt himself getting upset. He didn't want to hear any more about life as a tree frog. Fred yelled up in an angry voice, "Danny, could you be quiet up there? You're giving me a headache!"

"Oh, I'm sorry," Danny said. He felt sad and hurt. He sat quietly.

8

Danny heard Fred and climbed down a few branches. He moved quickly and easily without falling.

"What are you doing, Fred?" he asked in a friendly voice.

"I was just finishing up my lunch," Fred answered. "How is life up high today, my friend?"

5

"It's wonderful!" Danny announced. He loved being a tree frog. He felt lucky to be able to climb this way and that. He had sticky pads on his hands and feet.

"I noticed today that my skin is the same color as these leaves. I had a great hiding spot!" Danny told Fred.

"Well, it is too bad I can't hop up there to play hide-and-seek with you, Danny," Fred said.

Sometimes Fred wished he could get up in the tree like Danny. Fred was a great jumper with powerful hind legs, but he couldn't climb trees. He was much too big.

Suggested levels for Guided Reading, DRA,
Lexile,® and Reading Recovery™ are provided
in the Pearson Scott Foresman Leveling Guide.

Moving Day

by Marianne Lenihan
illustrated by Victor Kennedy

Genre	Comprehension Skills and Strategy
Humorous fiction	• Plot and Theme • Realism and Fantasy • Summarize

Scott Foresman Reading Street 2.4.4

ISBN 0-328-13287-X

9 780328 132874

90000

Vocabulary

block

chuckle

fair

giant

strong

tears

trouble

Word count: 379

Note: The total word count includes words in the running text and headings only. Numerals and words in chapter titles, captions, labels, diagrams, charts, graphs, sidebars, and extra features are not included.

Reader Response

1. In a sentence or two, tell what the plot of this story is. Use a chart like the one below to organize your answers.

Beginning

↓

Middle

↓

End

2. What do you think the main idea of this story was? What details help you know?

3. Do you think the cat is right on page 5 when he thinks, "This isn't fair!"?

4. Why was the move difficult for the cat? In what ways do you think moving could be difficult for people?

Services and Providers

All the people in a community depend on one another. You need others and they need you.

In this story the Smith family depended on the movers. They needed the movers to help them. The movers were providing a service to the Smiths.

What other kinds of community services can you think of that people provide and use?

Moving Day

by Marianne Lenihan
illustrated by Victor Kennedy

PEARSON

Scott Foresman

Editorial Offices: Glenview, Illinois • Parsippany, New Jersey • New York, New York
Sales Offices: Needham, Massachusetts • Duluth, Georgia • Glenview, Illinois
Coppell, Texas • Ontario, California • Mesa, Arizona

"Where have you been silly cat?"
I heard Mrs. Smith calling at last. She
picked me up and put me in the cat
carrier. I *hate* the cat carrier.

*Well, at least they didn't leave
without me. Phew!* I thought at last.

Finally, the van doors closed. The movers pulled away from the house. Everyone had forgotten about me. *Thank goodness!* I thought with a chuckle.

I hid outside in the neighborhood all afternoon. Then I started to get worried. Where were the Smiths?

It all happened on a foggy Saturday morning. My life was turned upside down and inside out. You probably know the trouble I'm talking about if your family has ever moved.

Let me back up. You see, I'm the Smith family's cat. Now cats don't like changes. This is Dim, the Smiths' dog. Dogs will go anywhere with anyone at anytime. But not me. I think there's no reason to change where you live.

None of this slowed down the movers. They picked up the boxes and threw them outside. The boxes landed in the bushes and the flowerbeds. All my favorite places to hide were ruined. Then it started to rain. I *hate* rain!

Boxes were stacked along the walls in tall blocks. I had to duck behind them. I did not want to get tossed around!

Just then Dim came into the room. He was jumping and wagging his tail. Then . . . you guessed it! Down came all the stacked boxes like an earthquake.

One night at dinner, my family decided that we needed to move. They thought we needed a bigger home.

I thought, *What's wrong with this house? This isn't fair.* I wished cats could get tears in their eyes. Then I could show them how upset I was. But I just sat looking sad.

So we were going to move, and that was that. Old Dim was delighted. I wanted to swat his nose!

Then it happened. The movers arrived before sunrise. They brought giant boxes and carts on wheels. I was so scared I could hardly move.

I watched and listened from the highest shelf in the family room. The strong movers looked like jugglers from a circus. Everything was flying through the air. Crash! Smash! Crunch!

6

7

Watch Out!

by Donna Foley

Genre	Comprehension Skills and Strategy	Text Features
Narrative nonfiction	• Fact and Opinion • Main Idea • Ask Questions	• Labels • Glossary

Scott Foresman Reading Street 2.4.5

PEARSON
Scott Foresman

scottforesman.com

ISBN 0-328-13290-X

9 780328 132904

90000

illustrated by Burgandy Beam

Vocabulary

angry

branches

clung

fingers

picnic

pressing

special

Word count: 504

Reader Response

1. On page 6, what is the difference between the campers' and Dave's opinion of stormy weather?

2. What are some questions you had about the weather while you read this book?

3. On page 8, Jackie shows how weather is measured using *special* tools. Why are they *special*? Make a web like the one below to brainstorm special tools a weather forecaster uses.

4. How does the photo on page 13 help you understand what a wind gauge does and what it looks like?

Glossary

angry *adj.* feeling upset or mad.

branches *n.* parts of the tree that grow out of the trunk.

clung *v.* held tightly to someone or something.

fingers *n.* five end parts of your hand.

picnic *n.* party outdoors with a meal.

pressing *v.* pushing something in a steady way.

special *adj.* unusual or different in some way.

Watch Out!

by Donna Foley

illustrated by Burgandy Beam

PEARSON

Scott Foresman

Editorial Offices: Glenview, Illinois • Parsippany, New Jersey • New York, New York
Sales Offices: Needham, Massachusetts • Duluth, Georgia • Glenview, Illinois
Coppell, Texas • Ontario, California • Mesa, Arizona

Dave's campers have learned a lot about the weather today! They learned how storms happen. They learned how tools are used to measure changes in weather conditions.

Some of the campers now agree with Dave. Weather changes can be interesting and fun. What do *you* think?

ISBN: 0-328-13290-X

We measure how much rain has fallen with a rain gauge. It is a metal cylinder. Rain falls into the gauge. Then we can see how much rain fell.

Rain gauge

Dave is a summer camp counselor. Today the campers are going on a field trip to the weather station near the beach. First they are planning a picnic under the trees.

Some campers climbed the trees. They clung to the branches with their fingers. Dave tells the campers that the branches are like a giant umbrella. Their shade can keep everyone cool. It can protect them from getting sunburned.

A wind gauge measures the speed of the wind. A wind gauge has three or more cone-shaped cups. These cups turn. The number of turns per minute tells us the speed of the wind.

Wind gauge

We use two instruments to measure the wind. A weather vane is used to show which way the wind is blowing. If a weather vane points south, that means the wind is blowing toward the south.

Weather vane

Suddenly a strong breeze begins to blow. Dark clouds start rolling in. Big raindrops fall from the sky. Dave tells everyone to run to the boathouse for shelter. He explains it is not safe to stay under the trees in a storm. Lightning can strike the trees.

Some of the campers feel upset and angry. Their picnic was cut short by the storm. Dave says that as long as they are safe, stormy weather can be interesting and fun to watch. They can investigate the weather station now!

A barometer has a small, airless container with a pointer, or needle. The needle moves up or down as the air pressure outside the container changes.

Today there was a drop in air pressure before the storm started. This shows that stormy weather is coming.

Barometer

As hot and cold air move, they make changes in air pressure. Air pressure means air pressing down on Earth. We measure air pressure with a barometer.

Dave takes his group to meet Jackie, the lifeguard. One of her jobs is to keep track of storms and other changes in the weather. Jackie records what the weather is like in charts and logs. This helps her do her job of keeping swimmers and other people on the beach safe.

Knowing how weather works is important. People like Jackie measure the weather with special tools. Jackie describes what is happening with the air, sun, wind, and water.

Let's look at today's storm. How did it happen? We measure temperature with a thermometer. A thermometer tells us how hot or how cold the air is.

When air gets hot it is light. Hot air rises. This leaves a gap. Cold air rushes in to replace the rising hot air.

Thermometer

Suggested levels for Guided Reading, DRA,
Lexile,® and Reading Recovery™ are provided
in the Pearson Scott Foresman Leveling Guide.

Social Studies

Social Studies

Who Can Help?

Genre	Comprehension Skills and Strategy	Text Features
Expository nonfiction	• Main Idea • Cause and Effect • Text Structure	• Headings • Glossary

Scott Foresman Reading Street 2.5.1

PEARSON

Scott
Foresman

scottforesman.com

ISBN 0-328-13293-4

9 780328 132935

90000

by Donna Foley

Word count: 588

Reader Response

1. What is the main idea of this book?

2. How did the author organize the information in this book? How did the headings help you as you read?

3. Two of the words on page 12 end in –ly. Find those words and read them aloud. Use each word in a complete sentence.

4. What new information did you learn that you didn't know before? What would you still like to know about community workers? Use a chart like the one below to record your answers.

What I learned	What I want to know

Glossary

buildings *n.* houses, apartments, or places where people live, work, or play.

burning *v.* on fire.

masks *n.* coverings that people wear to protect their faces.

quickly *adv.* with speed.

roar *v.* to make a loud sound like a lion.

station *n.* a central place where people gather.

tightly *adv.* securely.

Who Can Help?

by Donna Foley

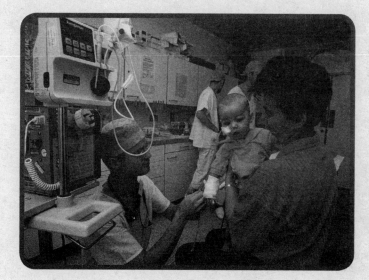

PEARSON

Scott Foresman

Editorial Offices: Glenview, Illinois • Parsippany, New Jersey • New York, New York
Sales Offices: Needham, Massachusetts • Duluth, Georgia • Glenview, Illinois
Coppell, Texas • Ontario, California • Mesa, Arizona

On the way to the hospital, EMTs call the nurses and give them information about what the patients need. Nurses and doctors wait for the ambulance. They rush patients to the emergency room.

Now the community workers have done their jobs. The patients are safe!

Every effort has been made to secure permission and provide appropriate credit for photographic material. The publisher deeply regrets any omission and pledges to correct errors called to its attention in subsequent editions.

Unless otherwise acknowledged, all photographs are the property of Scott Foresman, a division of Pearson Education.

Photo locators denoted as follows: Top (T), Center (C), Bottom (B), Left (L), Right (R), Background (Bkgd)

Opener: ©DK Images;1 ©DK Images;3 Getty Images; 4 Getty Images; 5 Getty Images; 6 ©DK Images; 7 Getty Images; 8 ©DK Images; 9 Borkoski, Matthew/Index Stock Imagery; 10 (B) ©DK Images, (C) Tony Freeman/PhotoEdit; 12 ©DK Images; 13 ©DK Images; 15 Getty Images

ISBN: 0-328-13293-4

2 3 4 5 6 7 8 9 10 V010 14 13 12 11 10 09 08 07 06 05

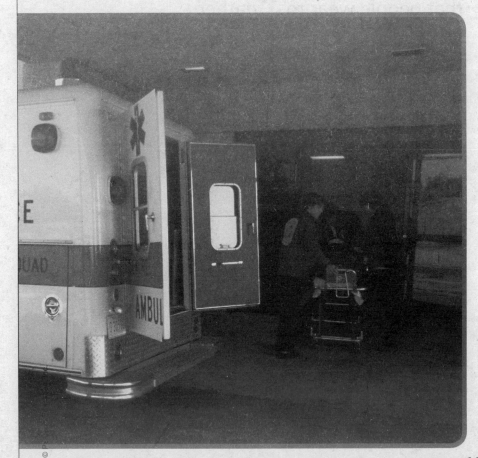

Police also respond to the call for help. They block off traffic to keep other people away from the fire. Police officers help firefighters and EMTs do their work safely. Without police officers keeping things safe, the firefighters and EMTs would have a lot more things to worry about.

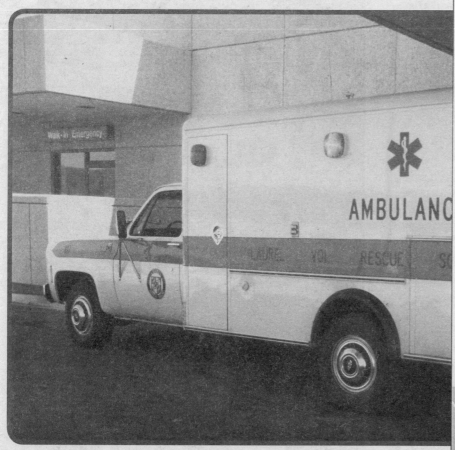

Community workers include 911 operators, EMTs, firefighters, police officers, nurses, and doctors. They all work together to help people in danger. Together, they keep their community safe. Let's learn about how these community workers make our lives better.

911 Operators

Emergency line operators, or 911 operators, answer phone calls from people in danger. They keep the caller calm and ask the right questions. They make sure help gets sent out **quickly.** The 911 operators make sure that other people on the emergency team know everything they need to know to help.

The firefighters wear **masks** to protect themselves from the smoke. They put on their masks and enter the burning building. The firefighters carry people out of the building and hand them over to the EMTs. The EMTs check the patients and drive them to the hospital.

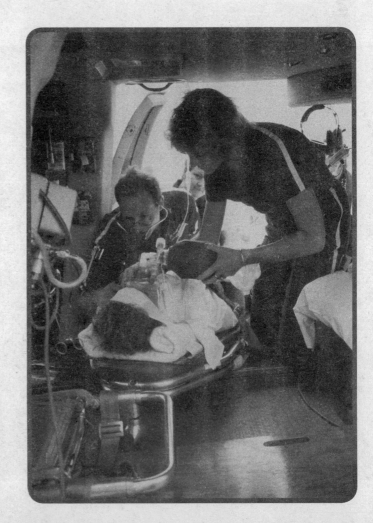

At the fire **station** the firefighters put on their gear and jump on the fire engine. Their sirens **roar.** The firefighters hold on **tightly.** Once they get to the fire, the firefighters pull out their hoses and spray the fire with water. They need to work quickly to save lives.

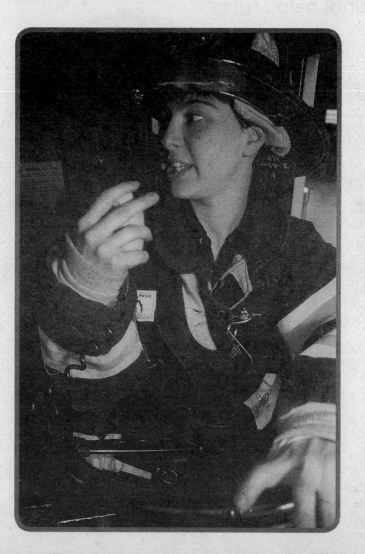

EMT Workers

An EMT is an emergency medical technician. EMTs pick up sick and hurt people and take them to the hospital. EMTs drive ambulances and get people to the hospital quickly. EMTs make sure people get the best care before a doctor or nurse can see them.

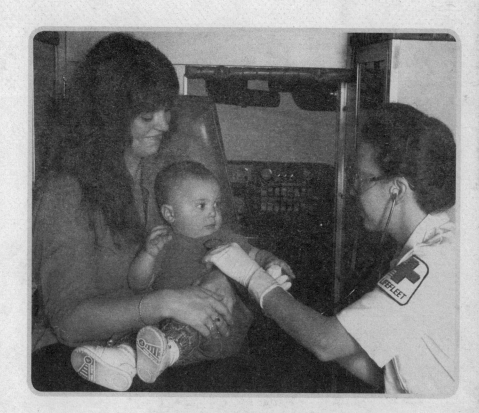

Firefighters

Firefighters help people caught in a fire. They can help people get out of **burning buildings.** Firefighters can save peoples' houses and belongings. Even when there isn't a fire, firefighters can sometimes use their equipment to help people in need.

The 911 operator then calls the police and the fire departments. She gives police officers and firefighters information about the person who needs help.

The 911 operator also has the important job of keeping the caller calm until help arrives.

In an Emergency

All the people you have learned about work together to help people in need. Let's see how they do their jobs in an emergency.

In an emergency a person dials 911. The 911 operator takes the call and finds out what kind of emergency it is.

Police Officers

Police officers serve and protect the people in their communities in many ways. Some police officers stop people from hurting themselves and others. Other police officers make sure drivers are driving safely. Police officers make sure everyone follows the community's rules.

Nurses and Doctors

Nurses usually work in a hospital. They help patients, doctors, and EMTs. They can help care for people who are elderly, sick, or hurt. Nurses make sure doctors get important information. They help people stay safe when the doctor is not around.

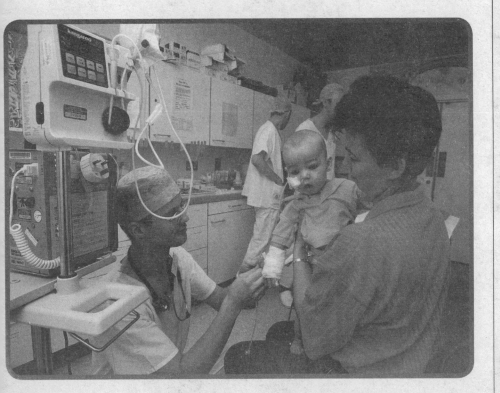

Doctors help people who are sick. Some doctors operate on people who are seriously hurt. Doctors give people medicines that can help cure their illnesses. Doctors also help teach people how to take care of themselves so they can stay healthy.

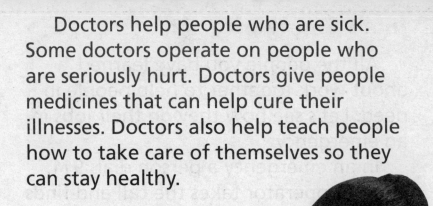

Science

Science

Life Science

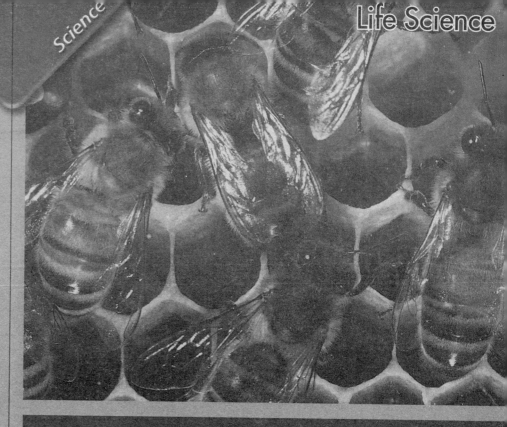

Animal Shelters

by Lindsay Auten

Genre	Comprehension Skills and Strategy	Text Features
Expository nonfiction	• Sequence • Author's Purpose • Graphic Organizers	• Captions • Headings • Glossary

Scott Foresman Reading Street 2.5.2

PEARSON

Scott
Foresman

scottforesman.com

ISBN 0-328-13296-9

90000

9 780328 132966

Reader Response

1. Which animal did you read about first? Next? Last?

2. The author talks about many kinds of animal shelters. Make a web like the one below to list all the different shelters you have learned about.

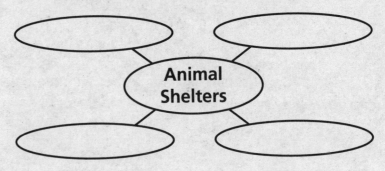

3. What does the word *flashes* mean? Use it in a sentence.

4. How do the pictures in this book help you understand what *shelters* are?

Glossary

flashes *n.* sudden brief lights.

lightning *n.* a flash of electricity in the sky.

pounds *v.* hits hard.

pours *v.* drops down.

rolling *adj.* having a deep loud sound

storm *n.* a strong wind with heavy rain, snow, or hail.

thunder *n.* a loud noise from the sky that comes after lightning.

Animal Shelters

by Lindsay Auten

Editorial Offices: Glenview, Illinois • Parsippany, New Jersey • New York, New York
Sales Offices: Needham, Massachusetts • Duluth, Georgia • Glenview, Illinois
Coppell, Texas • Ontario, California • Mesa, Arizona

No matter where they live, animals need shelter. There are almost as many kinds of shelters as there are kinds of animals, but all shelters have a very important job. They keep animals safe.

Every effort has been made to secure permission and provide appropriate credit for photographic material. The publisher deeply regrets any omission and pledges to correct errors called to its attention in subsequent editions.

Unless otherwise acknowledged, all photographs are the property of Scott Foresman, a division of Pearson Education.

Photo locators denoted as follows: Top (T), Center (C), Bottom (B), Left (L), Right (R), Background (Bkgd)

Opener: Library of Congress; 3 (Bkgd) Getty Images, Library of Congress; 4 (Bkgd) Getty Images, ©DK Images; 5 (Bkgd) Getty Images, Library of Congress; 7 Getty Images; 8(Bkgd) Getty Images, Library of Congress; 9 Library of Congress; 10 Library of Congress; 12(Bkgd) Getty Images, Library of Congress; 13 Library of Congress; 14(Bkgd) Getty Images, Library of Congress; 15 Library of Congress

ISBN: 0-328-13296-9

Shelter for Pets

Pets also need places where they can be protected and kept safe. Guinea pigs and hamsters need a special soft material called bedding to sleep in. Fish and lizards like to hide behind rocks.

This pet gecko needs a shelter that has twigs for climbing.

Many living things protect themselves from the weather. This protection is called shelter. During a **storm** the **rolling thunder,** the **flashes** of **lightning,** and the rainwater that **pounds** and **pours** down can be scary! You probably prefer to watch the storm from somewhere safe, dry, and warm.

Animals, large and small, also need shelter from the weather. Different animals prefer different kinds of shelter. Animals that are cared for by people, such as pets and farm animals, usually live in shelters made by people. Wild animals normally make their own shelters. But sometimes people help wild animals find shelter.

People can make shelters for wild animals. Look at this nice birdhouse.

Have you ever thought about building a birdhouse? Some small birds like to build nests inside birdhouses. You might also put out a bird feeder. Just remember to keep it filled! Bird feeders and birdhouses will attract birds to your yard.

Birds use nests for shelter. Many birds build their nests with twigs and leaves. Some birds use mud. Birds use their nests and birdhouses to hide from animals that hunt, such as cats, dogs, and snakes.

Farm Animal Shelters

Many farm animals use special buildings called barns for shelter. It is important to keep farm animals safe from hot and cold weather, and from other animals. What kinds of animals can you think of that live in barns?

Some people might think pigs roll in the mud because they like to get dirty. In fact, pigs roll in the mud to cool themselves off during hot weather. The wet mud protects the pigs' skins from the sun. Pigs like to have shelters near cool mud or under trees. This way they can keep out of the heat.

Wild Animal Shelters

Wild animals live in different kinds of homes. Bees live in a hive. Bees use the hive to protect their babies and to store honey. Bees must store their honey for the colder months. During the winter there are no flowers in bloom for bees to get food.

Chickens need care and protection too. They need sheltered places to lay their eggs. Chickens have feathers to keep them warm, but they do not like very cold weather. They can get frostbite if they are not kept warm enough. Farmers use heat lamps to keep their chickens warm.

Shelters for chickens are called chicken coops.

Just like pigs, cows need shelter from the weather too. Cows need shade in the summer and protection from icy wind in the winter. Cows look for trees in the fields, or pastures, where they graze to get shade. In the winter, most cows stay indoors.

Cows that do not live in a pasture need to be fed eight times a day. They are fed with corn or hay. Cows drink a lot of water too.

Cows can be kept in buildings. The buildings need to let in enough air for the cows to stay healthy. Some buildings have sprinklers to keep the cows cool.

Sheep can live in tough climates, but they still need shelter. Sheep have thick coats, called fleece. Their fleece grows very thick and keeps them warm through winter. In the spring, farmers cut off the sheep's fleece. This keeps the sheep cool. Sheep shelters are called sheep pens.

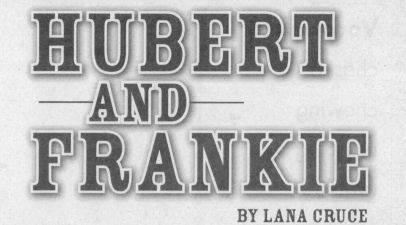

HUBERT
—AND—
FRANKIE

BY LANA CRUCE

ILLUSTRATED BY TOM LABAFF

Genre	Comprehension Skills and Strategy
Animal fantasy	• Theme and Plot • Compare and Contrast • Prior Knowledge

Scott Foresman Reading Street 2.5.3

PEARSON
Scott
Foresman

scottforesman.com

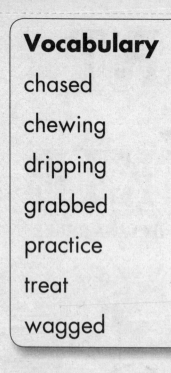

Vocabulary

chased

chewing

dripping

grabbed

practice

treat

wagged

Word count: 572

Reader Response

1. What is the big idea of this story? What events happened in this story? Use a chart like the one below to record your answers.

   Big Idea: ....

Beginning

   ↓

Middle

   ↓

End

2. What do you already know about dogs that helped you understand the story better?

3. *Chase* is a word that tells how someone moves. What other words can you think of that tell how someone moves?

4. Who do you think worked harder, Hubert or Frankie? Why?

Learning the Rules

Learning to listen and follow rules is an important part of being responsible. In this story, Hubert, who already knows the rules, helps Frankie learn to behave.

Part of being responsible can be helping those who are younger learn the rules. Can you remember a time when you helped someone younger than you learn a rule? Why did you do this? How did it make you feel?

HUBERT AND FRANKIE

BY LANA CRUCE
ILLUSTRATED BY TOM LABAFF

PEARSON
Scott
Foresman

Editorial Offices: Glenview, Illinois • Parsippany, New Jersey • New York, New York
Sales Offices: Needham, Massachusetts • Duluth, Georgia • Glenview, Illinois
Coppell, Texas • Ontario, California • Mesa, Arizona

ISBN: 0-328-13299-3

© Pearson Education, Inc.

Frankie's behavior got better every day. He listened when he heard his name. Hubert and Frankie agreed that their favorite things to do were to take a walk with the Kents, and then take a nap on the rug.

Once in a while, Frankie still chased the cat. After all, he was just a puppy!

"How did you learn to listen, Frankie?" Madeline asked. Frankie ran over to Hubert and put his paw on Hubert's paw.

"Hubert taught him!" said Madeline. Hubert barked happily. The Kent family was very proud of Frankie and Hubert. Mrs. Kent gave both dogs a treat.

Hubert had lived with the Kent family for a long time. He liked to go for walks and take naps. Frankie was the new puppy in the family.

Hubert thought Frankie was trouble. Frankie chased the cat and liked chewing on shoes. Hubert knew better than to do those things. He knew how to listen.

At first, Madeline thought the things that Frankie did were funny. Then Frankie grabbed and chewed her baseball glove. Madeline did not find this funny. It was not funny when Frankie left a half-chewed bone in Mr. Kent's shoe.

"Frankie is learning to listen!" said Mr. Kent. "Maybe he can learn some tricks after all! Maybe he can learn how to sit." Frankie sat as fast as he could.

"How did he learn that?" asked Mrs. Kent. "Did you teach him, Madeline?"

"I tried, but he wouldn't listen," Madeline said.

Suddenly, Madeline dropped her hamburger. It landed close to Frankie's nose. Frankie reached out to lick it.

"No, Frankie!" Madeline said. Frankie stopped right away. The Kent family all stopped talking and stared at Frankie.

Madeline tried and tried to teach Frankie to sit. Frankie would not listen. Madeline kept trying. Frankie just chased his tail. He rolled over on his back. He tried to lick her. He did everything except listen.

"I give up," said Madeline.

The next day Mrs. Kent found Frankie digging in the garden.

"Frankie, no!" she yelled. Frankie wagged his tail and went right on digging. Mrs. Kent patted Hubert on the head.

"You are a good dog, Hubert," she said. "But Frankie just does not listen."

During dinner that night, Hubert and Frankie sat waiting by the table. Hubert wanted to show everyone that he had taught Frankie how to listen. Frankie wanted to show off all the things he had learned.

No one was paying attention. The Kents were too busy talking.

6

11

Hubert and Frankie practiced all afternoon. Frankie learned his name and what the words *no* and *stop* meant. Hubert taught Frankie to sit, lie down, and stay.

"This is fun, Hubert," Frankie barked, licking Hubert's nose.

Hubert thought about when he was a puppy. He did not always listen either. It was hard to understand what Mr. and Mrs. Kent were saying. It took a long time to learn what their words meant. Hubert thought that he might be able to help.

Hubert looked for Frankie. Suddenly Frankie came racing into the room, dripping muddy water everywhere.

"STOP!" Hubert barked. Frankie stopped. He looked surprised.

"You have to learn to listen, Frankie." Hubert took Frankie out into the yard.

"The first thing you have to learn is your name," woofed Hubert. "Your name is Frankie. When someone says your name, you have to listen. Now let's practice." Frankie nodded his head. His ears flopped up and down.

Suggested levels for Guided Reading, DRA,
Lexile,® and Reading Recovery™ are provided
in the Pearson Scott Foresman Leveling Guide.

Social Studies

You Can Make A Difference!

by Laura Crawford

illustrated by Aleksey Ivanov

Genre	Comprehension Skills and Strategy	Text Features
Narrative nonfiction	• Author's Purpose • Draw Conclusions • Ask Questions	• Labels • Glossary • Headings

Scott Foresman Reading Street 2.5.4

PEARSON

Scott Foresman

scottforesman.com

ISBN 0-328-13302-7

9 780328 133024

90000

Vocabulary

adventure

climbed

clubhouse

exploring

greatest

truest

wondered

Word count: 686

Note: The total word count includes words in the running text and headings only. Numerals and words in chapter titles, captions, labels, diagrams, charts, graphs, sidebars, and extra features are not included.

Reader Response

1. How do you think the author hopes you will use the information in this book?

2. If you could write to the students in the Cans for Kids club, what questions would you ask them? Make a web like the one below to brainstorm.

Cans for Kids

3. Find the words *greatest* and *truest* in the glossary of this book. Use each of these words in your own sentence.

4. If you could start an adventure, what kind of adventure would you like it to be?

Glossary

adventure *n.* an unusual or exciting thing to do.

climbed *v.* went up using hands and feet.

clubhouse *n.* a building used by a group of people for a special reason.

exploring *v.* traveling to discover new areas.

greatest *adj.* best and most important.

truest *adj.* most real, right, or loyal.

wondered *v.* wanted to know about.

You Can Make A Difference!

by Laura Crawford

illustrated by Aleksey Ivanov

Editorial Offices: Glenview, Illinois • Parsippany, New Jersey • New York, New York
Sales Offices: Needham, Massachusetts • Duluth, Georgia • Glenview, Illinois
Coppell, Texas • Ontario, California • Mesa, Arizona

Illustrations by Aleksey Ivanov

ISBN: 0-328-13302-7

Are *you* ready to help? Here are some simple things you can do every day.
- Pick up your litter.
- Find ways to make less trash.
- Don't forget to recycle your cans.

You can work with other people too. Your **truest** friends will always be ready to help you. How about building a **clubhouse** where you can meet to think of ways to help in your neighborhood?

Teaching Others

One of the **greatest** goals of the Environmental Protection Agency is to teach children about reducing, reusing, and recycling. The EPA hopes children will learn these three R's and help teach other people about them.

Making a Difference

Do you like nature? Does your family recycle? Are you a litterbug? Where does your garbage go?

These are things every person needs to think about. Don't leave protecting the environment up to your mom and dad. It's your job too! Even young people can make a big difference. Have you ever **wondered** how?

The environment is all the land, water, and air in our world. The Environmental Protection Agency, or EPA, is a group of people who work hard to keep the environment healthy and clean. Kids can help the EPA in its work in important ways.

Let's look at some projects that kids have been involved in.

Cans for Kids

Cans for Kids is a group of adults and kids who started a big **adventure** collecting cans. They sell the cans to an aluminum company for recycling. Since the group started their project, they have collected more than seven million cans! Cans for Kids gives the money they get for the cans to high school students. The money helps high school students pay for college.

The parents agreed to pack lunches with as little waste as possible. When packing lunches, parents reused the plastic containers each day. This way the students did not need to throw away five plastic sandwich bags each week.

Contract

We want to keep the world beautiful, so we agree to use and reuse our plastic containers. We also agree not to use plastic bags.

Parents: Children:

Protecting Animal Habitats

One group of students wanted to make the wetlands in their neighborhood a healthier place. The students planted four hundred trees. They also placed bird boxes around the wetlands area. The students hoped this would bring more birds to their neighborhood.

The next year, the students planted eight hundred more trees. They added bat boxes and bird boxes. They provided homes and food for these animals. The third year, they planted even more trees around the wetlands! Today, students continue to take care of the trees. They also check and repair the bat and bird boxes.

Bird box

Bat box

At one school, students decided to try making less garbage. They started a waste-free lunch program. The staff gave the students reusable lunch boxes. The students used fewer plastic bags and wrappers. This way everyone made less garbage.

They did not just find paper and cans. They picked up rugs, televisions, beds, and a dishwasher! They collected 310 bags of garbage and more than three hundred old tires. The group worked for a long time to get rid of the dangerous and dirty trash. All of this trash was thrown away properly or recycled.

Saving Animals in Danger

Another group of students was worried about the birds in their town. These students offered to help at an animal center. They took care of birds and other animals that had been hurt. The students spent their weekends and time after school working at the center.

The vets at the center showed the students how to bathe and walk the animals. The students held a food drive to collect food for stray animals.

Rabies is a dangerous disease. A vet can give animals a shot that keeps them from getting rabies. The students helped the center set up a rabies clinic. The clinic workers gave rabies shots to many cats and dogs.

Making Less Waste

Another group of young people noticed a lot of litter in their town. They decided to work together to make their local roads cleaner. They got garbage bags, put on gloves, and began **exploring.** They collected garbage along the roads. They **climbed** up roadsides. What do you think they found?

Freda's Signs

by Debbie O'Brien

illustrated by Victor Kennedy

Genre	Comprehension Skills and Strategy
Humorous fiction	• Realism and Fantasy • Theme • Monitor and Fix Up

Scott Foresman Reading Street 2.5.5

PEARSON

Scott
Foresman

scottforesman.com

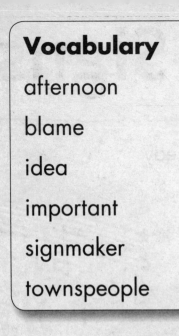

Vocabulary

afternoon

blame

idea

important

signmaker

townspeople

Word count: 528

Reader Response

1. Think about what happened in the story. Use a chart like the one below to give examples of what could or could not happen in real life.

Could Really Happen	Could Not Really Happen

2. What mistakes did Freda make with the words on her signs? Reread the story to help you remember Freda's mistakes.

3. Who were some of the townspeople in this story?

4. What could Freda have done to avoid the problems she had with the signs?

Safety on the Streets

Before Garrett A. Morgan came along, busy streets were full of cars, bicycles, animal-drawn wagons, and pedestrians. They all shared the streets—without traffic lights! Accidents happened all the time.

Morgan decided to solve the problem. He invented a traffic signal. It signaled when to stop and go. It helped pedestrians to cross streets more safely. The modern traffic lights of today are based on Morgan's ideas.

Freda's Signs

by Debbie O'Brien
illustrated by Victor Kennedy

PEARSON

Scott
Foresman

Editorial Offices: Glenview, Illinois • Parsippany, New Jersey • New York, New York
Sales Offices: Needham, Massachusetts • Duluth, Georgia • Glenview, Illinois
Coppell, Texas • Ontario, California • Mesa, Arizona

16

So Freda fixed all the signs. Soon the town of Midvale was back in order. Freda became the town's official signmaker.

And now she always reads the list before she even picks up her paintbrush.

Mayor Martin said gently, "I guess you learned your lesson."

"I sure did," said Freda. "I'll get the list. I'll fix all the signs."

The mayor said, "I knew you would do the right thing, Freda."

The people of Midvale needed new signs around town. Who could do the job? Everyone was busy—except Freda.

The problem was that Freda was very forgetful. But Mayor Martin and the townspeople decided to give her a chance.

Mayor Martin gave Freda a list of the new signs to be made. "Follow this list carefully," he told her.

Freda was excited to be Midvale's signmaker. She knew it was an important job. When Freda got home, she put the list on her kitchen table.

Mayor Martin called Freda to his office. He asked, "Freda, did you use the list I gave you for the signs?"

Freda looked down. "No," she gulped. "I forgot to bring it with me."

The townspeople told Mayor Martin about the problems all over town.

"Do you have any idea who is to blame for all this?" the mayor asked.

"It's Freda," the townspeople told him. "Tell her to stop!"

On the morning of the job, Freda woke up late. She rushed into town on her bike. When she got there, she realized she had forgotten to bring the mayor's list.

"Oh, well," sighed Freda. "I am sure I can remember all the words."

So Freda began to work. The first sign was at the bus stop. Freda wrote *Bug Stop*.

"Look," said an ant. "This sign says we must stop here."

So the ants stopped. Soon many bugs were lined up at the sign.

The dogs were confused. They were also quiet.

"What's the idea? Why can't we bark?" one dog asked. "That's what we learned in school."

"Read the sign, my friend," answered another dog. "We have to obey it."

The people in cars were confused too. They parked everywhere. They caused a traffic jam.

That afternoon Freda worked on another sign. It was near the Acme Watchdog School. Dogs were trained to bark there. Several dogs watched as Freda made the sign.

Freda finished the sign. She posted it in front of the school. It said *No Barking*.

That was a problem for the townspeople.

"We cannot get near the bus stop because of all the bugs," some people complained.

"And now the buses don't know where to stop!" cried others.

Freda was already making the next sign. She posted it in front of City Hall. It said *Keep On The Grass.*

The townspeople read the sign. Soon, they were walking, running, and biking everywhere, right on the grass!

The park ranger came running. She was waving her hands above her head. "Oh no!" she exclaimed in a loud voice. "Don't crush the grass! Stay on the paths."

"But the sign says to keep on the grass," the people responded. And they continued walking, running, and biking on the grass.

Social Studies

Women in Baseball

by Carl Thomas

Genre	Comprehension Skills and Strategy	Text Features
Expository nonfiction	• Compare and Contrast • Cause and Effect • Visualize	• Captions • Glossary

Scott Foresman Reading Street 2.6.1

PEARSON

Scott
Foresman

scottforesman.com

ISBN 0-328-13308-6

90000

9 780328 133086

Vocabulary

athlete

bases

cheers

field

plate

sailed

threw

Word count: 611

Reader Response

1. Compare women's baseball before 1948 and after 1948. Make a chart like the one below to show what changed. Did anything stay the same?

Before 1948	After 1948

2. Reread page 6. Close your eyes and make a picture in your mind of what the words describe. What do you see?

3. What does the author mean by the word *sailed* on page 13?

4. Reread page 5. How do you think the beginning of World War II affected baseball?

Glossary

athlete *n.* a person trained in sports.

bases *n.* in baseball, spots marked by bags to which players run after they hit the ball.

cheers *n.* shouts of support from fans for a team.

field *n.* the area where athletes play or compete.

plate *n.* the starting place in a baseball game.

sailed *v.* moved fast.

threw *v.* sent into the air using the hand and arm.

Women in Baseball

by Carl Thomas

PEARSON

Scott Foresman

Editorial Offices: Glenview, Illinois • Parsippany, New Jersey • New York, New York
Sales Offices: Needham, Massachusetts • Duluth, Georgia • Glenview, Illinois
Coppell, Texas • Ontario, California • Mesa, Arizona

Every effort has been made to secure permission and provide appropriate credit for photographic material. The publisher deeply regrets any omission and pledges to correct errors called to its attention in subsequent editions.

Unless otherwise acknowledged, all photographs are the property of Scott Foresman, a division of Pearson Education.

Photo locators denoted as follows: Top (T), Center (C), Bottom (B), Left (L), Right (R), Background (Bkgd)

Opener: Layne Kennedy/Corbis; 1 © Comstock Inc.; 3 (TR, CL) Brand X Pictures; 4 Denver Public Library, Western History Collection; 5 Brand X Pictures; 6 Harry M. Rhoads/Denver Public Library, Western History Collection; 7 (C) Bettmann/Corbis, (B) Brand X Pictures; 8 Brand X Pictures; 9 Bettmann/Corbis; 10 (T, B) Brand X Pictures; 11 (L, CR) image100; 12 (CL) Brand X Pictures, (C) image100; 13 (C, B) image100; 14 (BL) © Comstock Inc., Rudi Von Briel/PhotoEdit; 15 Layne Kennedy/Corbis

ISBN: 0-328-13308-6

2 3 4 5 6 7 8 9 10 V010 14 13 12 11 10 09 08 07 06 05

Girls playing in Little Leagues led to a new professional baseball team for women. It was formed in 1994. It was called the Colorado Silver Bullets. The Silver Bullets played against men's teams for three years. The Silver Bullets showed once again that baseball is not just for boys or men. It is for everyone!

In 1998 Ila Borders became the first woman to start as pitcher in a minor league baseball game.

Softball became popular when women's baseball leagues ended. But women never gave up their hope of playing professional baseball again.

Until 1974 only boys were allowed to play on Little League teams. This made creating teams for women's baseball difficult. Today, girls are joining Little Leagues all around the world.

When you think of baseball do you imagine men hitting home runs and scoring at home **plate?** Remember that many women play baseball too! Did you know that women's baseball teams took to the **field** as early as 1866? Women have been playing baseball for more than one hundred years.

In the 1890s women's baseball was very popular. Hundreds of teams played across the country. For more than forty years, thousands of women enjoyed the thrill and the challenge of baseball. Sadly, however, the fans' **cheers** did not last. By 1934 the women's teams were gone. Men's minor league teams replaced them.

Then, she **threw** it in as one of the fastest players **sailed** around the **bases**. The player was trying to make a triple. She was tagged out and never made it to third base.

© Pearson Education, Inc.

In the summer of 1996, women's softball became an Olympic sport. Softball is one of the most popular sports in the world for women today.

Follow the action in these photos. The ball was hit high into the air. The outfielder made a great catch.

In the 1940s many men went off to fight in World War II. Most women did not go. In 1943 the All-American Girls Professional Baseball League was started. There were four teams that played in major league baseball parks. It was the first time in history that women were allowed to play baseball professionally.

Baseball team from the early 1900s

The teams played 108 games in the first season. The top two teams played for the championship of the league. Almost two-hundred thousand people cheered the efforts of these ballplayers. At the time, that was a huge number of fans!

Even after the professional softball league for women ended in 1980, women continued to play the game. Women's softball became so popular it was part of the Pan-American Games in 1979. Colleges across the country started to form women's softball teams.

Professional baseball for women ended after 1954, but the athletes continued to play. Women started to play softball. Softball was invented in Chicago in 1887. The first international championship for women's softball happened in 1965. A professional women's softball league was started in 1976. It lasted for four years.

The first season was a great success. Two more teams joined the league in the second season. Players tried out for teams that spring. Each **athlete** was hoping for the chance to play the game she loved. The league continued to do well. The future for women's baseball looked bright.

Spring training for the teams in the league

Official Softball

The league continued to grow and attract new fans. Many people paid to see the women play. In 1946, ten thousand people went to watch one game. In 1948 more fans went than ever before. Over nine-hundred thousand people filled the ballparks.

After 1948 women's baseball became less popular. People slowly stopped going to see the women play. Without money from ticket sales, the teams could not pay their players. Some teams went out of business. By 1954 only five teams could finish the season. The league ended soon after that.

Coach and players from the All-American Girls Professional Baseball League, 1944

Social Studies

Heroes OF THE American Revolution

Genre	Comprehension Skills and Strategy	Text Features
Biography	• Fact and Opinion • Compare and Contrast • Monitor and Fix Up	• Captions • Maps • Glossary

Scott Foresman Reading Street 2.6.2

PEARSON
Scott
Foresman

scottforesman.com

by Joe Adair

Vocabulary

America

birthday

flag

freedom

nickname

stars

stripes

Word count: 626

Note: The total word count includes words in the running text and headings only. Numerals and words in chapter titles, captions, labels, diagrams, charts, graphs, sidebars, and extra features are not included.

Reader Response

1. Sybil Ludington was the bravest hero of the American Revolution. Is this a fact or an opinion? Explain your answer.

2. Reread the section on Benjamin Franklin. He did many amazing things in his life. Make a web like the one below to list the things Benjamin Franklin did.

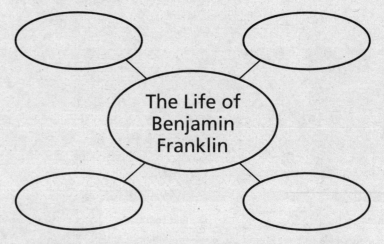

The Life of Benjamin Franklin

3. Explain why the Fourth of July is called America's *birthday*.

4. Look at the map on page 3. How is it different from maps of the United States we normally see today?

Glossary

America *n.* a name people use for the United States of America.

birthday *n.* the day a person was born or something was started.

flag *n.* a piece of colored cloth with symbols on it.

freedom *n.* being free; the ability to think, do, say, or believe as you please.

nickname *n.* a name used instead of a real name.

stars *n.* pointy shapes that stand for the stars we see in the sky.

stripes *n.* long thin lines of color.

Heroes OF THE American Revolution

by Joe Adair

Editorial Offices: Glenview, Illinois • Parsippany, New Jersey • New York, New York
Sales Offices: Needham, Massachusetts • Duluth, Georgia • Glenview, Illinois
Coppell, Texas • Ontario, California • Mesa, Arizona

16

The Fourth of July is the **birthday** of the United States. On July 4, 1776, the American Colonies first declared their freedom from Britain. The men and women who fought during the American Revolution helped America gain this freedom. We remember these heroes every year on the Fourth of July.

Today, there are 50 stars for 50 states. The 13 stripes remind us of the 13 colonies.

© Pearson Education, Inc.

The Flag and the Fourth

During the American Revolution, the first **flag** of the new America was made. This flag had thirteen **stars** for the thirteen colonies. Today, the American flag has fifty stars and thirteen **stripes**. The stars stand for the fifty states. The stripes stand for the thirteen colonies of the past.

On the original American flag, there were 13 stars, one for each of the 13 colonies.

The Thirteen Colonies

In 1775 **America** did not have states. Instead, America had thirteen colonies. These colonies were ruled by a country called Great Britain. Great Britain was far away. Great Britain's king did not know what the colonies were like.

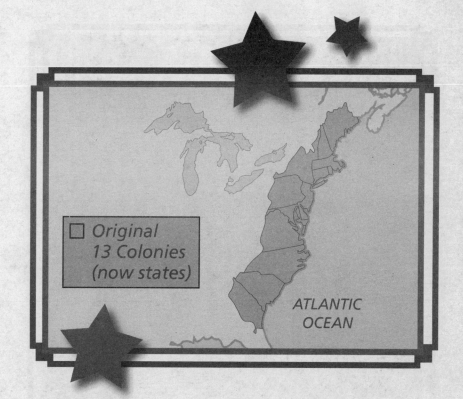

Original 13 Colonies (now states)

ATLANTIC OCEAN

America was very different in 1775. There were only thirteen colonies.

In 1775 trouble started between Great Britain and the Thirteen Colonies. Great Britain was taking tax money from the Colonies. The colonists did not want to pay this money. There were other problems too. The American Revolution began.

Colonists got angry at unfair British taxes.

Sybil Ludington was a hero at 16. She rode her horse all night to call American soldiers together to save her burning town.

Dicey Langston earned the **nickname** "Daring Dicey." When she was just 15, she heard British soldiers planning an attack. She walked all night and crossed a wide river to warn the Americans.

This statue honors Sybil Ludington and her daring ride. The stick in her hand was the only protection she had.

Margaret Corbin went to war with her husband, John. John Corbin was in charge of a cannon. When John was shot during a battle, Margaret quickly took his place. She continued to fire the cannon until she was wounded too. Margaret Corbin was later honored by the new United States government.

Women fought during the American Revolution.

Many Americans wanted to be independent from Great Britain. They were willing to fight for their **freedom**. Everyone who fought to make America free was a hero. But there were some special people worth remembering.

Benjamin Franklin

Benjamin Franklin was born in Boston in 1706. He wrote books and invented useful things. He invented the first swim fins. He also invented special glasses to help people see better. Benjamin Franklin also studied science. His work helped people understand how lightning and electricity work.

Franklin experimented with electricity.

Some Surprising Heroes

You may be surprised to know that women, and even some children, fought in the American Revolution. A woman named Deborah Sampson wanted to join the fight for freedom. She dressed like a soldier and joined the army. She fought in many battles. She later wrote about her experiences during the war.

Deborah Sampson dressed as a soldier during the American Revolution

The last really big battle of the American Revolution is called the Battle of Yorktown. French soldiers and sailors helped the Americans in this battle. On October 19, 1781, the Bristish soldiers gave up and asked for the war to end. George Washington was a very smart general. He is remembered as a hero of the American Revolution.

George Washington led Americans to victory.

During the American Revolution, Benjamin Franklin was sent to Europe. He asked France to help the colonists. He asked for guns for the American army. Benjamin Franklin spent many years helping to win the war against Great Britain. He worked to make America free. He is a hero of the American Revolution.

Benjamin Franklin is cheered as a hero.

George Washington

George Washington was born in Virginia in 1732. He is known as the "father of our country." He became the first President of the United States. Before he was President, George Washington was in charge of the army during the American Revolution.

A statue of the first President of the United States

The war was not easy. George Washington and his troops faced two very hard winters. They were very cold. They did not have enough food. George Washington did not let his troops give up. He fought hard to help America win the war against Britain.

American troops cross the Delaware River.

Lexile,® and Reading Recovery™ are provided
in the Pearson Scott Foresman Leveling Guide.

Social Studies

Birthdays Around the World

by Marilyn Greco

Genre	Comprehension Skills and Strategy	Text Features
Narrative nonfiction	• Draw Conclusions • Compare and Contrast • Summarize	• Captions • Glossary • Headings • Map

Scott Foresman Reading Street 2.6.3

PEARSON

Scott
Foresman

scottforesman.com

ISBN 0-328-13314-0

90000

9 780328 133147

Vocabulary

aunt

bank

basket

collects

favorite

present

Word count: 795

Reader Response

1. What information from this book makes you think that "Happy Birthday" is sung in many languages all over the world?

2. People eat special foods on their birthdays. Make a web like the one below to help you summarize the types of foods at birthday parties in this book.

3. Of all the presents you have received, which one is your favorite? Why?

4. Which birthday activity in this book do you think you might like to try? Why?

Glossary

aunt *n.* your mother or father's sister, or your uncle's wife.

bank *n.* a place where people keep their money.

basket *n.* something to carry or store things in.

collect *v.* to gather or bring things together.

favorite *adj.* the thing you like better than all the others.

present *n.* a gift.

Birthdays Around the World

by Marilyn Greco

Editorial Offices: Glenview, Illinois • Parsippany, New Jersey • New York, New York
Sales Offices: Needham, Massachusetts • Duluth, Georgia • Glenview, Illinois
Coppell, Texas • Ontario, California • Mesa, Arizona

Every effort has been made to secure permission and provide appropriate credit for photographic material. The publisher deeply regrets any omission and pledges to correct errors called to its attention in subsequent editions.

Unless otherwise acknowledged, all photographs are the property of Scott Foresman, a division of Pearson Education.

Photo locators denoted as follows: Top (T), Center (C), Bottom (B), Left (L), Right (R), Background (Bkgd)

Opener: DK Images; 1 (C, Bkgd) Getty Images; 3 (Bkgd) Getty Images, (C) DK Images; 4 DK Images; 5 DK Images; 6 ©Comstock Inc.; 8 (B) DK Images, (T) ©Comstock Inc.; 9 Getty Images; 10 ©Comstock Inc.; 12 DK Images; 13 DK Images; 14 (TL) DK Images, (BL) ©Comstock Inc.; 15 (TL, BR) ©Comstock Inc., (CL) DK Images

ISBN: 0-328-13314-0

2 3 4 5 6 7 8 9 10 V010 14 13 12 11 10 09 08 07 06 05

Everywhere, people have different celebrations to honor their friends and relatives for different reasons. Do you celebrate your mom or dad on Mother's or Father's Day? What about Grandparent's Day? What are some other celebrations in your country? Shouldn't everyone get to feel special on their day?

ILYA, Russia

YOSHIKO, Japan

VICTOR, Philippines

© Pearson Education, Inc.

In this book you learned about how children in the United States, Russia, Mexico, the Philippines, and Japan celebrate birthdays. There are special treats, and the birthday boy or girl may get presents, sing songs, or play games.

Faces and Places Around the World

AISHA, United States

ROSA, Mexico

A birthday celebrates the day on which you were born. Everyone has a birthday. Many people around the world celebrate birthdays with special treats and activities. Children worldwide spend their special day in different ways.

United States

Hi! I'm Aisha, and I live in the United States. Today I am turning seven. My birthday is my **favorite** day of the year. My friends and family are coming to our house to celebrate with me. We are going to share a birthday cake with seven candles and play lots of games. My friends will bring me gifts. I'm going to have fun!

At my party, all of us made birds. We folded them from special small, pretty, paper squares. Making things by folding paper is called origami. I really like it. My friends gave me the birds they made. Birds mean good luck in Japan. I think my next year will be very lucky!

Origami birds

Japan

My name is Yoshiko, and I just turned seven today. Today has been a great day! Seven is an important age in Japan. My mother made a special meal of beans and rice. She made a cake too. Lots of people came to see me and brought me presents. My aunt gave me a beautiful Japanese dress, called a kimono, to wear to special events.

Dad will cook food on the grill outside. Mom and I will blow up lots of colorful balloons. We will play Pin the Tail on the Donkey. At the end of the day, I'll give each of my friends a bag with a surprise in it. It's a tiny bubble maker. Shhhh! Don't tell anyone!

Pin the Tail on the Donkey

5

Russia

Hi! I'm Ilya, and I live in Russia. Yesterday was my seventh birthday. It was great! I woke up and found a **present** in a **basket** on the chair by my bed. My **aunt** had made a card for me. In Russia we eat a special birthday pie. My mom baked it and carefully wrote my name in the crust.

After dinner, we'll play a game called Cat and Dog. All the players, except one, are "cats." The other player is a "dog." The dog guards some imaginary bones and the cats try to steal the bones without getting tagged. I love being a cat because I'm fast!

At night I will open my gifts. I might get books, toys, or money. If I get money my mom will put it in the **bank** for me.

A "Happy Birthday" song in Tagalog, a language of the Philippines

Maligayang bati,

Maligayang bati,

Maligayang bati sa iyo,

Maligayang bati mahal na (name).

I'm Victor, and I live in the Philippines. A seventh birthday is an important birthday where I live. Today we are going to have a big feast. Grandpa is roasting a large pig. He says eating meat on your birthday brings good luck.

I can't wait until the party starts. People will bring presents, and I will **collect** them at the door. I will give everyone a small party favor too. It's going to be a balloon or a party horn.

My family and friends came to my celebration. For fun we all wore hats and masks, and played a singing game called "The Round Loaf." My friends made a circle around me and let me have the first turn. I felt special all day. I can't wait to turn eight next year!

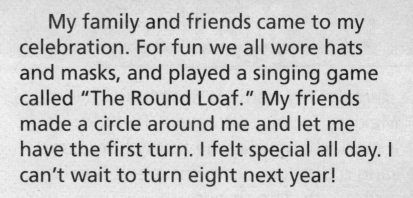

Party mask

Mexico

Hola! My name is Rosa, and I live in Mexico. Today I am seven. This morning a mariachi band came to my home and sang a birthday song for me. It is called a *serenata*. The singers were my uncles and cousins. They woke me up! Then my grandma invited everyone in for breakfast.

Piñata

Later, we had a big party with a *piñata*. A piñata is made of colorful paper. My piñata was filled with candy, nuts, and little toys. My dad hung the piñata in a tree, and we all took turns swinging the bat at it. It was hard because my mom tied a scarf over our eyes.

When the piñata burst, the goodies flew everywhere, and my friends and I scrambled to pick them up! My mom also made a cake called Three-Milk Cake. I made three wishes when I ate my piece, but I can't tell you what my birthday wishes are. If I do, they might not come true!

COWBOY DAYS

by Joanna Korba

Genre	Comprehension Skills and Strategy
Historical fiction	• Cause and Effect • Character • Graphic Organizers

Scott Foresman Reading Street 2.6.4

PEARSON

Scott
Foresman

scottforesman.com

ISBN 0-328-13317-5

9 780328 133178

90000

illustrated by Jerry Tiritilli

Word count: 926

Reader Response

1. The invention of barbed wire caused ranchers to be able to put up fences. What effect did this have on Carl's life?

2. People still work on ranches today, but many things are different. Make a chart like the one below, showing how things have changed.

Past	Present

3. A compound word is a word made up of two smaller words. One compound word in this story is *cowboy*. It is made up of the words *cow* and *boy*. What other compound words can you find in the story?

4. If you wanted to be in a Little Britches rodeo, what do you think you would need to be able to do?

Rodeos for Kids

Back in the old days, cowboys used to get together and have contests. It was something to do for fun after they got back from a trail drive or after a roundup. Rodeos grew out of these contests. They started in the late 1880s as a place where cowboys could show off their skills to others.

These days, there are cowgirls in rodeos too. There are even some rodeos just for kids! The oldest kids' rodeo is run by an organization called Little Britches. It's for kids from five to eighteen years old. Do you think you would like to try being in a rodeo?

COWBOY DAYS

by Joanna Korba
illustrated by Jerry Tiritilli

PEARSON

Scott
Foresman

Editorial Offices: Glenview, Illinois • Parsippany, New Jersey • New York, New York
Sales Offices: Needham, Massachusetts • Duluth, Georgia • Glenview, Illinois
Coppell, Texas • Ontario, California • Mesa, Arizona

Illustrations by Jerry Tiritilli

ISBN: 0-328-13317-5

I'm going to leave
the old ranch now.
I've got no place
to roam.
They've roped and fenced
my cattle range.
And the place don't
feel like home.

There are still some cattle ranches around today. The people working on ranches rope cattle, fix fences, and take cattle to market. Things are different now than they were in Carl's day.

People use machines to fix the fences. They use trucks to move the cattle. People working on ranches now are called cowhands, not cowboys. A lot more cowhands are women these days.

As for me, I don't know if I'll work on the ranch, but I'll never forget about Carl Grigsby and the rest of the cowboys. Sometimes, I sing a song Carl used to sing, way back when he was still a cowboy. It's about the end of the open range, when the fences came to Texas. It goes like this:

My name is Jeannie Grigsby. I want to tell you about my great-great-great-great-uncle, Carl Grigsby. He was born more than 150 years ago, and he was a cowboy.

I've been hearing family stories about Uncle Carl since I was born.

When Carl Grigsby was just sixteen, he went to work for the Lazy L Ranch in Texas. Mr. Tom Lambert, the ranch owner, raised a type of cattle called Texas longhorns.

Carl liked the longhorns. He said they were the best cattle around. They'd eat almost anything that grew.

The flat land all around the ranches was called the range. The range was wide open land. All the ranchers grazed their cattle on the range.

That sounded like much more fun than fixing fences. Everyone had always told Carl how good he was on a horse. He'd often beaten the other cowboys in races.

Carl Grigsby spent the rest of his life performing in rodeos. When he got too old to perform, he'd come and watch the big rodeos. He'd remember the old days, when he was a real cowboy.

Carl worked around the ranch, taking care of the cattle and fixing the fences that he hated. He didn't feel like a cowboy anymore. He felt like a misfit.

One day, a ranch hand told him about something called a rodeo. It was a kind of show where cowboys showed their skills riding and racing horses, and roping and handling cows and calves.

Each rancher put his cowboys in charge of his cattle. The cowboys had to keep their herd together on the range.

Carl and the other cowboys from the Lazy L rode out each morning. They'd watch over the longhorns all day and keep them from mixing with other cattle from a different ranch.

The most important job for cowboys was the trail drive. The trail drive was when a herd of cattle was taken to the closest railroad station. From there, the cattle went east to the market. It sounds like easy work, doesn't it? But it wasn't!

There could be as many as three thousand longhorns on the drive. That's a lot of cattle to watch over! A trail drive was not just a short little trip. At that time the nearest railroad to the Lazy L was in Dodge City, Kansas.

The next thing Carl knew, he was out in the hot midday sun pounding fence posts into the ground and stringing barbed wire. He thought fences were a big mistake.

"The range is for everybody," he'd say. "We should keep it open so we can all share it, not fence it in!"

Carl missed the open range, but he still rode on trail drives—until the railroad came to Texas a few years later. There was no need for cattle drives after that. The trains took the cattle to Dodge City without help from the cowboys. The days of the big trail drives were over.

When Carl had been working for the Lazy L for about ten years, something big happened. Barbed wire was invented.

People could unwind this wire and attach it to fence posts. This made it easy to put up long fences. Soon, ranchers were fencing in their land. The fences kept the cattle together. The ranchers didn't need cowboys to do that job anymore.

It could take three months to drive the cattle up the trail to Dodge City.

Carl and the rest of the cowboys had to keep the cattle together, headed in the right direction. Some cowboys would lead the way. Others would ride beside and behind the herd.

The cattle raised a lot of dust as they moved along. Carl wore a bandanna to try to keep some of the dust away from his face. But dust was always getting into his eyes.

If you asked Carl, "What's the worst thing that can happen on a cattle drive?" he would probably say, "STAMPEDE!"

A loud sound could sometimes scare the cattle. A clap of thunder would startle them. All of a sudden, they would gallop off in the wrong direction.

The cowboys would have to gallop out and get ahead of the stampede. They could sometimes see the cattle charging right at them!

The cowboys would rise up in their saddles, wave their hats, and shout. This would stop the cattle and make them turn back.

What do you think was the best thing about a trail drive? For Carl it was sitting around the campfire at sunset when the cattle were resting.

The cowboys would cook, eat, talk, and watch the sun go down. Sometimes they would sing songs until midnight.

Suggested levels for Guided Reading, DRA,™
Lexile,® and Reading Recovery™ are provided
in the Pearson Scott Foresman Leveling Guide.

A Special Festival

by Riley Obach

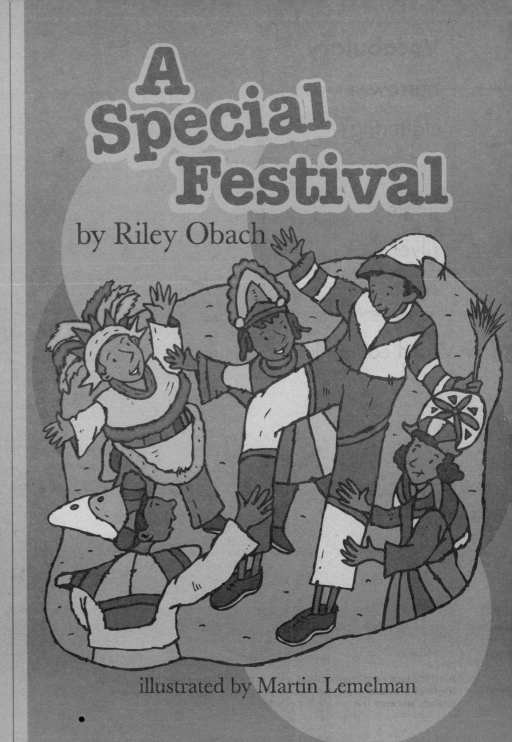

illustrated by Martin Lemelman

Genre	Comprehension Skills and Strategy
Realistic fiction	• Character, Setting, Plot • Sequence • Prior Knowledge

Scott Foresman Reading Street 2.6.5

PEARSON
Scott
Foresman

scottforesman.com

ISBN 0-328-13320-5

9 780328 133208

90000

Vocabulary

borrow

clattering

drum

jingle

silver

voice

Word count: 1,070

© Pearson Education, Inc.

Reader Response

1. In what settings does this story take place? What other setting does Zeke think about?

2. What do you know about families that helped you understand this story?

3. On page 13, you read about the clattering of the food carts. Based on what you know about *clattering*, write what *clattered* and *clatter* mean in the following sentences:

   • The pans clattered to the floor.

   • Those garbage collectors made such a clatter.

4. Think of a celebration you and your family enjoy. Using a chart like the one below, compare your family's celebration with the celebration in this story.

Celebration in the Story	My Family's Celebration

Drums Around the World

Drums are important to many cultures around the world. In Japan people study drumming for years to perform at temple ceremonies. Some Japanese drum groups are famous and travel all over the world.

Drums are important in much of Africa too. They are used for music and communication. Drum traditions in the Bahamas came from Africa.

Native Americans use drums for ceremonies and celebrations. At powwows men gather around a large drum, beating it and singing along.

Native American ceremonial drum

A Special Festival

by Riley Obach

illustrated by Martin Lemelman

PEARSON

Scott Foresman

Editorial Offices: Glenview, Illinois • Parsippany, New Jersey • New York, New York
Sales Offices: Needham, Massachusetts • Duluth, Georgia • Glenview, Illinois
Coppell, Texas • Ontario, California • Mesa, Arizona

Moments later, Zeke spotted Gramps. He was with his band from the Bahamas.

"Will you let me borrow a drum?" asked Zeke.

"No," said Gramps. But Gramps had a surprise for Zeke. Gramps had two goombay drums.

"I made this drum for you to keep, Zeke. I want you to play with our band."

"Wow! Thanks," Zeke said. "I guess Mom was right. She said I wasn't going to the Bahamas, but the Bahamas would come to me. Now I know just what she meant!"

And Zeke played his drum with Gramps's band as Dad and Mom followed along behind.

There was another surprise to come. Dad disappeared for a short time. When he came back, he was walking on stilts. He waved to Zeke from up above.

"Come and dance," he called to Zeke and Mom in a loud voice. They joined a dance line that was moving down the street.

Zeke kept looking for Gramps.

School was nearly out for the summer, and Zeke didn't know what he would be doing during vacation. Last summer had been very exciting for Zeke. He went to the Bahamas to visit Gramps, and it was one of the best summers of his life. It was the first time he had flown in an airplane. He went fishing with Gramps every morning. He helped cook fish over an open fire. He swam in the ocean every day. One night he even slept outside under the stars.

And if all that wasn't exciting enough, thanks to Gramps, Zeke's trip was full of music!

Gramps was a musician and played in a band. He played a drum called the goombay drum. Gramps showed Zeke how he had made the drum himself by stretching goatskin over a metal container.

When it was time to play, Gramps heated the drum to tighten the goatskin. It made the drum sound very deep. Zeke could not believe the sound of Gramps's drum.

Gramps let Zeke play the drum only at home. When the band played at parties, Gramps kept the goombay drum right by his side.

Mom and Dad unloaded the cans of conch chowder from the car. They brought them to a food cart. Other vendors were selling chicken and ice cream. Some vendors were selling arts and crafts.

On the street, bands were playing drums, horns, whistles, and bells. People everywhere were dancing to the lively music.

Zeke heard the bells jingle and the clattering of the food carts. He watched everything with wide eyes.

"Where are we going?" asked Zeke.

"We'll be there in ten minutes. Then you'll find out," Mom answered.

Just as Mom had promised, in ten minutes Dad parked the car. Zeke saw many people in bright costumes. There was music playing, and the smells of delicious food filled the air. It was a street festival!

"This is the Goombay Festival, Zeke," explained Gramps. "It's a festival that celebrates our Bahamian background."

Now a year had passed, and Zeke began to think about visiting Gramps again. As soon as summer vacation began, Zeke asked Mom, "Can I go to the Bahamas to see Gramps this summer?"

"No, not this summer, Zeke," said Mom, with a grin. Then she saw how disappointed Zeke looked. She added, "Maybe the Bahamas will come to you."

"What do you mean?" asked Zeke, but Mom wouldn't say anything more.

Later that day, Zeke asked Dad the same question, but Dad just answered, "Wait and see." Of course, that made Zeke even more curious. How could the Bahamas come to him?

What was even more mysterious was that Dad brought home some colorful cloth and bright feathers. Every night for a week, Zeke could hear Dad sewing on the machine.

What is going on? thought Zeke. He tried to find out what Dad was doing, but Dad kept him out of the sewing room.

6

Dad drove them home. When they got inside the house, he said, "Now everyone wait here. I have something special for you all."

Dad went into the sewing room. Soon, he came out with four bright costumes. He passed them out to Mom, Zeke, and Gramps. He held up the one for himself to show them.

"After you put on these costumes, meet me at the car," Dad said.

When Zeke got to the car, Mom and Dad were loading silver cans of conch chowder into the trunk. Gramps was already in the back seat with his goombay drum!

"Get in, Zeke," called Gramps. "Let's go."

11

When they got to the airport, Zeke found out why they were there. Gramps was just getting off a plane! Zeke ran to Gramps and hugged him.

"Gramps! I'm so happy to see you," said Zeke. Then he whispered, "Did you get my letter?"

"Yes," Gramps said. "I did get your letter."

"And what is the answer? Why was Dad sewing? Why was Mom cooking so much chowder?"

Gramps hugged Zeke. "You'll have to wait and see," he said.

"Oh no," groaned Zeke. Everything was still a mystery.

Mom's cooking in the kitchen was just as strange. She often made a small pot of conch chowder for the family's dinner. A conch is a kind of shellfish that you find in the Bahamas. But now Mom was cooking giant pots of chowder and storing silver cans of it in the freezer.

"Is the ocean running out of conch?" joked Zeke. "Who is going to eat all that chowder?"

Mom laughed but wouldn't explain.

Zeke couldn't get any clues from Mom and Dad about what they were up to. So he decided to write a letter to Gramps. Zeke was sure Gramps could help him figure out what his parents were doing.

Zeke mailed the letter and waited for an answer. But before Zeke could get a reply back from Gramps, the mystery got even more interesting.

On Saturday, Mom and Dad woke up Zeke very early. "Come on," said Mom. "Hurry and get dressed. We have a surprise. We're going to the airport."

Now Zeke was really confused. What did Dad's sewing and Mom's cooking have to do with going to the airport?

But Zeke went to the kitchen and sat down to breakfast. At least it wasn't conch chowder!

An hour later the family was in the car. Mom and Dad chatted the whole way. They talked about everything except why they were going to the airport.